LEGISLATION AND EDUCATION IN NORTHERN NIGERIA

LEGISLATION AND EDUCATION IN NORTHERN NIGERIA

by

ALBERT F. OGUNSOLA
Director of the Institute of Education,
Ahmadu Bello University, Zaria

1974
OXFORD UNIVERSITY PRESS
IBADAN . ZARIA

Oxford University Press, Ely House, London W. I
GLASGOW NEW YORK TORONTO MELBOURNE WELLINGTON
CAPE TOWN IBADAN NAIROBI DAR-ES-SALAAM LUSAKA ADDIS ABABA
NEW DELHI BOMBAY CALCUTTA MADRAS KARACHI LAHORE DACCA
KUALA LUMPUR HONG KONG TOKYO
Oxford House, Iddo Gate, P.M.B. 5095, Ibadan, Nigeria

ISBN 0 19 575237 4 (Limp edition)
ISBN 0 19 575237 6 (Cased edition)

Printed in Nigeria by The Caxton Press (West Africa) Ltd., Ibadan

FOREWORD

THIS BOOK has been the product of my study into the basis of Education Ordinances (1916-1966) as they relate to Education in Northern Nigeria. This study led to the award of the Ph.D. degree. The author was, however, encouraged by friends who read the thesis that he should consider publishing it for the benefit of teachers-in-training and those already in practice who would need to know about these Ordinances. In fact he was reassured that the book should appeal to the B.A./B.Sc. Education, P.G.C.E. and M.Ed. and Ph.D. students who are intending to go into the teaching profession. If the book can really serve this purpose, the author would definitely feel gratified.

The study consists of an historical survey of the background of Nigerian education, and a review of literature pertinent to the Nigerian education ordinances (1916-1966) which involved collection and organization of data, presentation of data and critical analysis of the data presented. Material was obtained from a study of pertinent literature, and from interviews and conferences with officials of the Ministries of Education in Northern Nigeria, and with experts on African Education in Nigerian, British and American Universities. Official documents in the National Archives in Kaduna, and in the Library of Congress in Washington were also consulted.

The findings which could be regarded as of major importance are:

(a) The objective of adaptation which dominated the development of education in Northern Nigeria for approximately fifty years and which influenced the educational legislation proved a failure. The most serious aspect of the failure being the wide gap it created between the supply of people at Independence in the North when compared with the South, who had the skill to operate the machinery of government as established by the colonial regime.

(b) Enrolment of primary-age children in school for the entire period has been greatest in those areas of Northern Nigeria where missionary schools have been encouraged by government permission and grants-in-aid. The ordinances have promoted and encouraged mission schools, and at the same time, expanded government-controlled schools in the same areas. They have not provided for a corresponding expansion of schools in the remaining areas of Northern Nigeria.

(c) The ordinances have given a greater degree of local control of primary education by establishing local education authorities. However, two limitations exist that are not normally found in countries influenced by Western-oriented education. In the first instance, local authorities are restricted to primary education. Secondly, local control is vested in the local authority.

(d) The ordinances established a system of financing education which incorporated different features of payment for each level of education, as well as for various sponsors of schools. This disparity is further evidenced in salaries and conditions of employment for teachers as between Ministry of Education employees, local authority employees and voluntary agency employees.

With these highlights in mind, it is the hope of the author that the significant role of the education ordinances will be recognized by all concerned.

It is quite possible that the education ordinances will continue to play more significant roles in our educational development. This will depend on the philosophies and policies we evolve to guide our education and the people who are henceforth to be in charge of the management of our schools.

CONTENTS

PART TWO

MAPS

DEFINITION OF TERMS USED

Regional government: the Federation of Nigeria before 1 April 1968 was divided into four parts, each of which was referred to as a region. The regions were: East, West, Mid-West and North. The regions have now been replaced by twelve states.

Native administration: means local government under the limited jurisdiction of a Nigerian ruler such as an Emir or a chief. The terms native administration and local administration have been used interchangeably.

House of Assembly: each of the four former regions of Nigeria had a legislative assembly known as the House of Assembly.

Civil service: is the term used to describe servants of the state or central government as civilians. It usually does not cover local government employees, nor staff of public corporations.

School Board: means a board established under the education ordinance with advisory functions on matters of education referred to it by the regional government.

Assisted school: is the term used in Northern Nigeria to designate a school that is partially supported by government grants-in-aid. A school not subsidized is referred to as an un-assisted school.

Voluntary Agency Schools: are schools operated by missionary bodies or other recognized bodies and are usually subsidized by grants-in-aid from the government.

N.A. Schools: are schools under direct control of the native authorities who are the local government. The schools are usually subsidized by the government through grants-in-aid.

Koranic schools: schools where children are taught by Mallams to learn the Koran by note. The schools are usually regarded as religious schools. The opening and closing of such schools has not been strictly controlled by law.

Government school: means a school owned and operated by the government.

Elementary school: means a vernacular day school in a town or village of Northern Nigeria in which a two-year syllabus was offered. The average age of entry was ten. The government disallowed this type of school after the 1956 Ordinance.

Primary school: means a boarding school in which education was given in the vernacular up to about the level of the English public standard VI. English was taught from the time of entry to all who had passed through the elementary school. The average age of entry was twelve. This type of school was also discontinued after 1956.

Primary school (after 1956): is an educational system with not less than ten pupils which offers a seven-year course. A child is admitted into the beginners' class at six.

Middle school: was a three-year course system beyond the primary school. This was discontinued after 1956 and replaced by the junior secondary school.

Standards I-VI: until 1956, when the term primary school was made applicable to both voluntary agency schools and native authority schools in the North, the voluntary agencies operated their schools on the syllabuses in use in Southern Nigeria. The course was an eight-year elementary school course broken down into Infants I and II and Standards I to VI.

Technical Institutes: are vocational schools.

Primary school teacher: is a teacher who by qualification and/or training is allowed by the Education Law of Northern Nigeria to teach any of the classes I-VII in a primary school.

Grade I teacher: has usually completed a Grade II course and had two or three years of academic and professional training. A Grade I certificate could be obtained by passing the external examination of London University, (G.C.E. 'A' level) and undergoing a practical teaching test.

Grade II teacher: usually a primary school level graduate who has had five years of academic and professional training.

Mallam/Arabist: usually a teacher literate in Arabic but with no professional training.

Grants-in-aid: an established system in Nigeria for giving grants to schools maintained by agencies other than the government to help buy school equipment and to pay teachers' salaries.

PART ONE

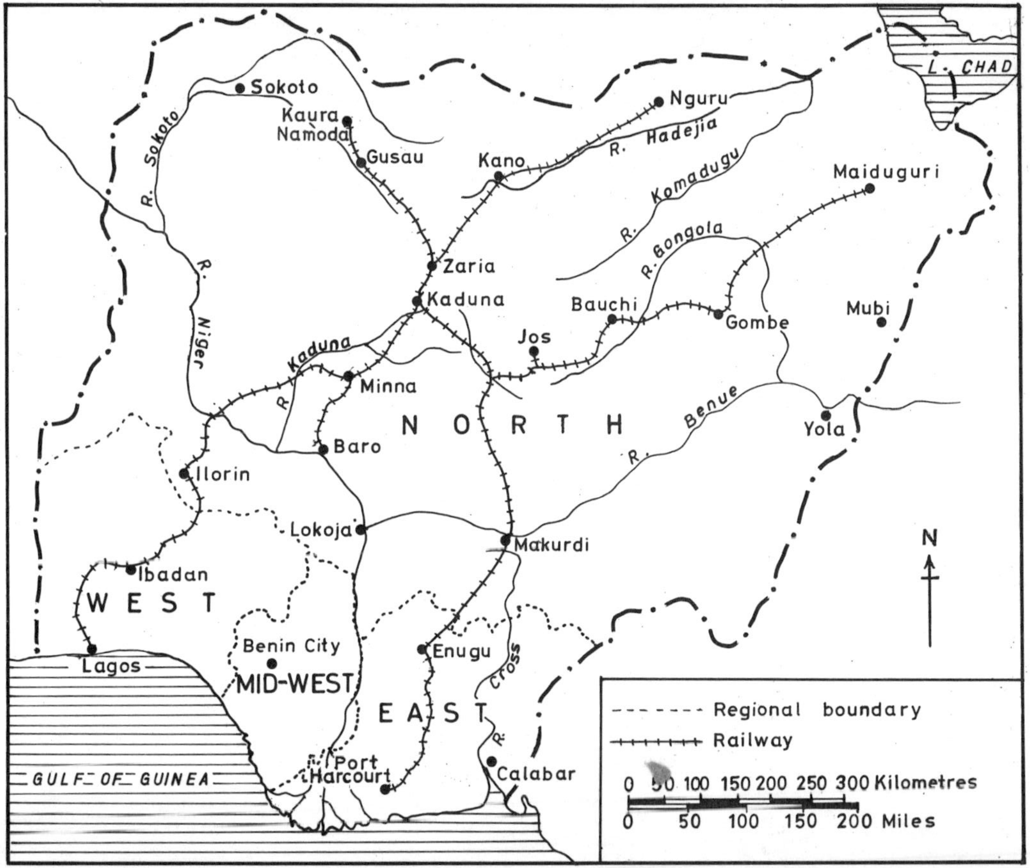
L. CHAD
Sokoto
Kaura
Namoda
Gusau
Kano
Nguru
R. Hadejia
R. Komadugu
Maiduguri
R. Sokoto
R. Gongola
Zaria
Kaduna
Bauchi
Gombe
Mubi
Jos
R. Niger
R. Kaduna
Minna
NORTH
R. Benue
Yola
Baro
Ilorin
Lokoja
Makurdi
N
Ibadan
WEST
Benin City
Enugu
Lagos
MID-WEST
Cross
EAST
R.
GULF OF GUINEA
Port
Harcourt
Calabar
Regional boundary
Railway
0 50 100 150 200 250 300 Kilometres
0 50 100 150 200 Miles

1

THE HISTORICAL BACKGROUND

MISSIONARY ACTIVITIES IN SOUTHERN NIGERIA

THE history of modern educational development in Nigeria dates from the coming of the Christian missions to the coastal areas of the southern provinces. Missionary activities in education can be traced back to the early sixteenth century, when in 1515 Portuguese missionaries visited Benin and obtained permission from the Oba of Benin to teach his son and the sons of a number of chiefs the rudiments of the Christian faith. In 1539, a Portuguese mission visiting Benin found a Christian Negro who was held prisoner by the Oba, teaching boys to read. The Portuguese seminary established at Sao Thome off the Nigerian coast in 1571, sent missionaries to Warri to teach the Itsekiris to read. But these early attempts were scattered and sporadic and so made no lasting impact as far as organized education was concerned.[1]

The first missionary contact in modern times in Nigeria was made by the Wesleyan Methodist Missionary Society which began its work in the coastal town of Badagry where it established a mission and built a school in 1842. This was in answer to the appeal made by James Fergusson, a Yoruba freed-slave who left Sierra Leone and came to settle at Badagry. In his letter dated 2 March 1841, to Reverend Thomas Dove, the Wesleyan missionary in Freetown who converted him to Christianity, Fergusson wrote as follows:

> So I humbly beseech you, by the name of Jehovah to send one of the messengers of God to teach us more about the way of salvation because I am now in a place of darkness where no light is. . . . . So I humbly beg of you that you . . . send us one of the servants of Christ to instruct us, by so doing, if we ourselves are well instructed, I will speak to them the same as I have been instructed.[2]

The Wesleyan Methodist Missionary Society and the Church Missionary Society were the first to respond to this appeal. In fact their agents arrived in Badagry within three months of each other. The King of Abeokuta where most of the freed slaves had settled invited Thomas Birch Freeman, the first Methodist Missionary to reach Badagry, to visit his town. Freeman entered Abeokuta on Sunday 11 December 1842. There he started a second mission station with a small school. In 1878 the Methodist Mission had advanced its educational work sufficiently to open a high school for boys and another for girls in Lagos.[3]

The Church Missionary Society comprised Bishop Samuel Crowther, a Yoruba who had been rescued by a British naval vessel from a slave-trading ship, a Mr. Townsend and the Reverend C.A. Golmer. They landed at Badagry from Sierra Leone and in 1846 they reached Abeokuta where they built a mission, a church and a school. By 1849 the Church Missionary Society Yoruba Mission had established four main stations at Badagry, Lagos, Abeokuta and Ibadan. This initial effort in Western Nigeria was followed by enterprises in the Niger delta and Eastern Nigeria. Bishop Crowther and his party visited Onitsha in 1857 and established a mission at Bonny in 1863. The Church Missionary Society had opened a teacher training institution at Abeokuta as early as 1849.[4]

In 1847, the United Free Church of Scotland set up a mission much further to the east at Calabar. It established vernacular schools along the rivers, and in 1895 opened the Hope Waddell Institute at Calabar which provided for trade and vocational training as well as for the training of teachers and pastors.[5]

In 1853, the American Southern Baptist Convention began work at Oyo; it founded the Baptist Academy at Lagos, and developed a vocational and trade school at Abeokuta.[6]

The Roman Catholic Mission established schools in Lagos in 1868 and in 1872 four Sisters from France organized education for girls. In 1876 the school now known as St. Gregory's College was founded. After penetrating the hinterland and establishing a mission station at Abeokuta in 1880, the mission extended its educational work over the Yoruba provinces. Asaba, which was in the western provinces, became a second focal point for such work. In 1885, a third Roman Catholic mission at Onitsha commenced educational activities in the eastern provinces.[7]

The Qua Iboe Mission, a Protestant society with its headquarters in Northern Ireland, was founded not far from Calabar. And in 1894, the Primitive Methodist Missionary Society came to the mainland from Fernando Po to spread its work over the Calabar and Owerri Provinces.

Beginning on the coast, most of the missions moved inland and along the main rivers and land routes, establishing their influence in many areas.

Hitherto, all the educational activities discussed have been mainly those of missions. It has become customary to divide the history of education in tropical dependencies into three phases: *(1)* the initial period of missionary activity, *(2)* the period of government interest, and *(3)* a period of change between the two. Much as this pattern appears attractive, it needs to be examined and applied carefully, since at no period did any one agency take full responsibility for education in Nigeria.[8] For many years the missionary societies working in the south of Nigeria had the field of education to themselves. But a few individual philanthropists, local governments, administrators and traders also paid some attention to the needs of education. The distinguishing element in the effort of the Christian missions was its persistent and expanding nature.[9]

MISSIONARIES IN NORTHERN NIGERIA

The activities of the Christian missions began much later in the North. They were greatly restricted by the fact that the Muslim Emirs of the North had, during the period of pacification, secured pledges from the government which made it difficult to admit the missions into the emirates without their consent.[10]

It is important to note at this juncture that when Europeans first came to Nigeria, especially Northern Nigeria, they did not find an educational vacuum. The Islamization of the northern parts of Nigeria had resulted in centres of intensive learning and religious activities in places like Sokoto, Katsina and Kano.[11] Before the establishment of the Protectorate of Northern Nigeria, Muslim schools were already functioning on a fairly wide scale. Most of these were Koranic schools where religious instruction was emphasized by Mallams able to read and write the Koran. There were in addition a few higher schools usually conducted by Alkalis and Imams. In 1913, the number of Muslim schools was estimated as 19,073, with a total attendance of 143,312.[12]

Into this complicated situation obtruded another factor—the advent of mission societies wishing to extend their fields into the new British possessions. In 1865, Bishop Crowther moved his mission station to Lokoja at the invitation of Consul Fell. In September of the same year, Bishop Crowther opened a school. It still exists today and is known as 'The Holy Trinity School'. A mission training college named 'Institution Causa Preparandi' was added in 1875 but made little progress and was discontinued in 1891.[13]

The Church Missionary Society's Niger Mission stationed at Lokoja was primarily concerned with the conversion of non-Muslims, but in May 1898 Lugard had been approached by Bishop Tugwell of the Church Missionary Society with a request for permission for a party of missionaries, who had studied in Tripoli and who wished to establish a Christian mission at Kano, to enter the new Protectorate. The Hausaland Mission was to be a mission to the Muslims.[14] This was the beginning of what later developed into an intensive government-missionary tangle over the education of the Muslims of Northern Nigeria.

The effective subjugation of the Northern emirates was not completed until the spring of 1903. This had taken Lugard three years; the next stage in the Protectorate's existence was the establishment of an efficient civil administration. Lugard wanted and needed the goodwill of the people of Northern Nigeria. Both in 1900 and 1902, Lugard had explained his policy of 'utilizing the abilities of this Fulani race, while putting an end to the tyranny and oppression which had hitherto marked their rule'. Furthermore, Lugard had declared the Fulani to be:

> ... unfit at present to exercise power except under supervision, nor do I hope for any great success in the present generation, but I hope and believe that with careful guidance their sons and grandsons will form invaluable rulers under British supervision and that their superior intelligence can be developed as a useful asset in our administration.[15]

It is quite clear that Lugard was at this time thinking of organized education for the sons of the chiefs in order to sustain his policy of 'Indirect Rule'. This partly explains why Lugard was prepared to allow the missions to extend their educational activities to Muslim areas despite his assurances of non-interference with their religion. Besides, it was cheaper to educate through the missions and there was also no precedent in West Africa for a government providing an education system.[16]

Permission was, therefore, given to Bishop Tugwell to establish a mission station at Kano on condition that:

> ... when the missionaries desire to penetrate beyond the zone into which the Administration can afford them effective guarantees of safety they should undertake in the clearest manner to attempt no advance without his consent and to be guided by the limitation which he may see fit to impose not merely for their own safety, but with the object of avoiding any violence which may involve the Administration.

The permission given to Tugwell was extended also to the Canadian, R.V. Bingham, who was the head of the African Industrial Mission later known as the Sudan Interior Mission.[17]

On 16 December 1899, the pioneers of the Church Missionary Society's Hausa Mission led by Bishop Tugwell and comprising Dr. W.R.S. Miller, the Reverends S.A. Richardson, J.C.D. Ryder and J.K. Burgin left England with the objective of reaching 'Kano or such other centre as God's providence may indicate', and they were bound by Tugwell's agreement with Lugard. The missionaries reached Jebba on 16 February 1900, and left the place on 5 March after they had failed to persuade the Emir of Ilorin to allow them to place a teacher in his city. They moved on to Kano through Daba and Wushishi without waiting for instructions from Lugard or any of his assistants. They arrived at Kano only to be turned out by the order of the Emir who believed them to be spies.[18]

The party retired to Zaria where the Emir gave them permission to live at Girku, outside Zaria town. Ryder died there and Richardson was invalided home to tell the story of the rebuff and hostility of the Emir of Kano. The rest of the missionaries decided to move on to Sokoto to see the Sultan. Colonel Lowry Cole who was in charge of the West African Frontier Force at Girku pleaded with them to desist from doing so. But Tugwell's reply was uncompromising, for he said:

> You are in no way responsible for us, we deeply appreciate your kind interest in us, but do not let us be a burden to you. Our service is rendered to the Ruler of the Kings of the earth—and therefore wherever we are, we are safe and therefore happy and confident.

Lugard intervened to stop them from going to Sokoto. This deadlock coupled with the treatment the missionaries received at Kano greatly strained the relationship between the administration and the missionaries. All the same, more missionaries arrived on the scene.[19]

In 1902, a Roman Catholic Mission of the Holy Ghost in Southern Nigeria wished to establish a mission at Ibi among the non-Muslims. Lugard gave permission for this. The mission also obtained permission to enter Bassa province, where the Church Missionary Society was already at work. By 1905 the mission had made little headway and it withdrew from Northern Nigeria.[20]

The Sudan Interior Mission, which was another rival to the Church Missionary Society, had acquired a site near Pategi at the confluence of the Niger and the Kaduna rivers. Its educational aims were industrial and agricultural and Lugard provided cotton seed for their farm. From Pategi the mission spread to Wushishi and Bida in 1903. The mission grew

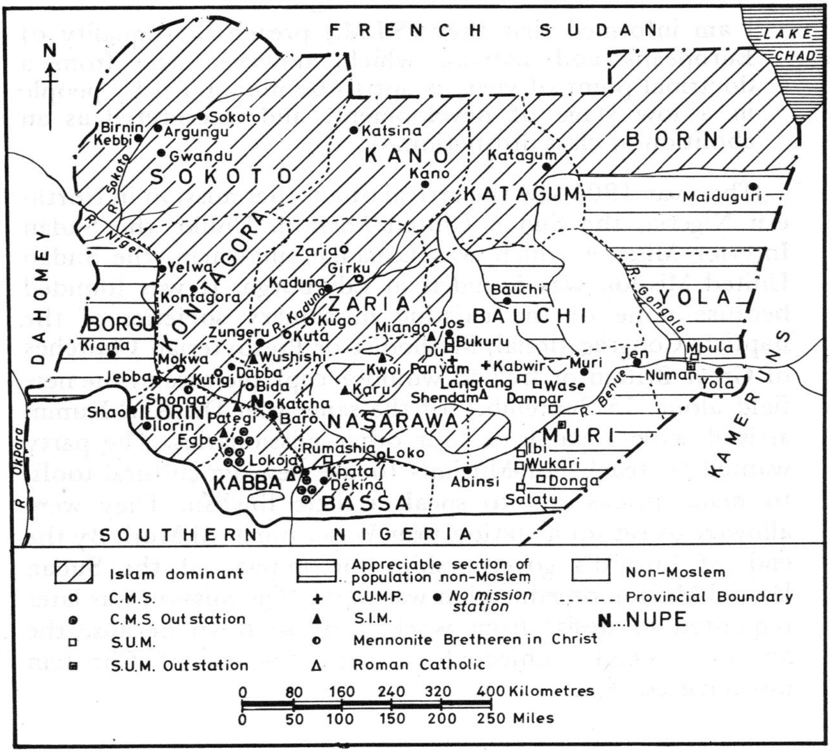
FRENCH SUDAN
LAKE CHAD
N
Sokoto
Birnin Kebbi
Argungu
Gwandu
SOKOTO
Katsina
KANO
Kano
Katagum
KATAGUM
BORNU
Maiduguri
R. Sokoto
R. Niger
DAHOMEY
Zaria
Girku
Yelwa
KONTAGORA
Kontagora
Kaduna
ZARIA
R. Kaduna
Bauchi
BAUCHI
YOLA
R. Gongola
BORGU
Kiama
Zungeru
Kugo
Kuta
Miango
Jos
Bukuru
Du
Mokwa
Wushishi
Kwoi
Panyam
Kabwir
Muri
Jen
Mbula
Jebba
Kutigi
Dabba
Bida
Karu
Langtang
Wase
Numan
Yola
Shonga
Katcha
Shendam
Dampar
Shao
ILORIN
Pategi
Baro
NASARAWA
R. Benue
Ilorin
Egbe
Rumashia
Loko
MURI
Ibi
Lokoja
Kpata
Wukari
KABBA
Dekina
Abinsi
Donga
BASSA
Salatu
KAMERUNS
R. Okpara
SOUTHERN NIGERIA
Islam dominant
Appreciable section of population non-Moslem
Non-Moslem
C.M.S.
C.U.M.P.
No mission station
Provincial Boundary
C.M.S. Out station
S.I.M.
N...NUPE
S.U.M.
Mennonite Bretheren in Christ
S.U.M. Outstation
Roman Catholic
0 80 160 240 320 400 Kilometres
0 50 100 150 200 250 Miles

vegetables successfully but because of boll worm, two-thirds of their cotton crop was lost. The industrial aims of the mission had no real success and so it concentrated on evangelization. Education was not much emphasized by the Sudan Interior Mission and they were not given much encouragement by the administration as Lugard was becoming suspicious of them. He once wrote as follows:

> I am informed that they (S.I.M.) preach the equality of Europeans and natives, which, however true from a doctrinal point of view, is apt to be misapplied by people in a low stage of development, and interpreted as an abolition of class distinction.[21]

The year 1904 saw the arrival of another mission in Northern Nigeria, the Sudan United Mission. Unlike the Sudan Interior Mission which was Canadian in origin, the Sudan United Mission was founded in Edinburgh. It was founded because none of the existing missionary societies of the Baptist, Congregational, Methodist or Presbyterian Churches of Great Britain or Ireland would accept the care of the new field alone. In September of the same year Dr. Karl Kumm arrived with a party of four other missionaries. The party wanted to teach non-Muslims to use new agricultural tools, to make bricks and to speak a little English. They were allowed to set up a station near Wase, north of Muri. By the end of Lugard's governorship, the impact of the Sudan United Mission on education was slight. The mission was later requested to desist from work in Wase town because the Muslim chief objected to the presence of Christian missionaries.[22]

THE ZARIA EXPERIMENT

So far, all the missionary organizations that ventured into Northern Nigeria concentrated on reaching the non-Muslims. Only the Hausaland Mission of the Church Missionary Society carried the message to the Muslims. The fact that in 1905 the mission was still the only mission to the Muslims placed it in a strong position for formulating plans to help carry out the intentions of Lugard for educating Mallams and sons of chiefs.

Miller produced the first detailed plan for this purpose. This has come to be known as the 'Zaria Experiment'. From this experiment it was hoped that (if successful) it would develop to fulfil the educational needs of the Protectorate recognized by both mission and administration.[23]

Miller dealt first with the class for literate Mallams. He suggested that the Emir of each province should be requested by the Governor to select two Mallams, versed in Koranic scholarship but preferably not courtiers. They should stay with him for six months and for the first three months receive lessons in reading and writing Hausa in Roman script. Afterwards they should receive three months instruction in elementary geography, grammar, arithmetic and hygiene including health and sanitation. Lessons were to occupy two hours and there was to be no religious instruction at that stage.[24]

Secondly, there was to be a boarding school for the sons of chiefs. Miller suggested that each Emir should be asked to send two sons or two children of important families in his province, aged 12-16 years. Each Emir was to pay whatever sum the Governor considered adequate for the support of the two boys and for the school materials which they used. The school was to be built on ground given by the Emir of whatever town was chosen by Lugard as the place of instruction.[25]

The idea behind the plan was that of a small inexpensive beginning from which Mallams might later be sent to begin primary schools in other provinces, thus enlarging the single school system; moreover, the welfare of the country would be promoted by the training offered to the next generation of Emirs.

Lugard indicated his approval of the plan, while praising the mission for its achievements, especially with Bida School. But then at that time Lugard's term of office was drawing to a close so he passed the final decision on to his successor, Sir Percy Girouard. Girouard submitted Miller's plan and Lugard's comments to the Residents for their comments.[26]

Meanwhile, Miller started his boys' school in May 1907. The Emir of Zaria chose fifteen boys from the leading families in Zaria town as the other Emirs sent nobody. The boarding school became a day school. The Emir of Zaria continued to show interest in the school. In fact when Miller ran into difficulties and wanted to close the school because of the indifference of many of the pupils, the Emir came to his rescue by weeding out the undesirables and left him with six keen pupils to each of whom the Emir presented a special robe. The six boys attended regularly and made progress. This later developed into Wusasa Day School. However, the boarding school for the sons of chiefs which Miller envisaged did not materialize.[27]

The Mallams' class fared better. One convert, Mallam Fate, was to prove a great help to Miller in all translation work. Another Mallam returned to his native town of Katsina after completing a course with Miller, and there gained the respect of the Emir for his increased knowledge and ability. It was one of Miller's Mallams who taught the Emir of Zaria to read Hausa in the Roman characters. Thus with the adults Miller was achieving the results for which Lugard had hoped.

In the meantime, all the Residents had replied giving reasons for opposing Miller's plan. The Colonial Office in London studied all the opinions including those of Miller in which he expressed his dismay at the Residents' opposition to his efforts. The Colonial Office decided to withdraw its support for Miller's activities and so sent the following telegram: 'I regret extremely that I gave any countenance to the project.'[28]

FAILURE OF THE EXPERIMENT

Following the new stand of the Colonial Office, from 1907 onwards the mission societies were to find it increasingly difficult to extend their spheres within Northern Nigeria, and the hope of the Church Missionary Society of developing mission education throughout the Muslim provinces was 'not only dead but damned'.[29]

The pattern of educational development in the south was one of expansion in which the missions were encouraged to spread into the interior while the pattern in the north was one of restricted expansion.[30] Both in the southern and northern provinces, the government was faced with the problem of the education of the Muslim children. It became more evident in the northern provinces, when the mission experiment was made to fail. For Miller not only blamed the Residents for the failure of his scheme but also maintained that:

> I could have done a great deal for the education of the country before the Education Department got into its stride much later on, but this again was feared to have elements which would excite the suspicion of the Moslem rulers.[31]

Henceforth it became the sole responsibility of the Protectorate Government to provide schools for the education of Muslims in the northern provinces. And there was unhealthy rivalry and badly planned educational expansion among the different missionary organizations in the south.[32] All combined led to direct government participation and involvement in education. It became necessary for the government not only to provide schools but also to make laws for the operation of schools and the regulation of missionary activities in the field of education.

NOTES

1 L. J. Lewis, *Society, School and Progress in Nigeria* (Oxford: Pergamon Press), p.23.

2 T. T. Solaru, *Teacher Training in Nigeria* (Ibadan University Press, 1964), p. 2.

3 Government Printer, *Annual Report of the Department of Education—1st April 1951 to 31st March 1952* (Lagos, Nigeria: Government Printer, 1954), pp. 5-6.

4 Lewis, op. cit., pp. 24-26.

5 Government Printer, Annual Reports, 1951-1952 loc. cit.

6 Lewis, op. cit., p. 27.

7 Government Printer, loc. cit.

8 L. J. Lewis, *Educational Policy and Practice in British Tropical Areas* (London: Thomas Nelson and Sons Ltd., 1954), p. 9.

9 Ibid., p. 10.

10 A. C. Burns, *History of Nigeria* (London: Allen and Unwin, 1929), p 259.

11 Desmond Wright Bittinger, 'An Educational Experiment in Northern Nigeria in its Cultural Setting' (Doctoral dissertation, University of Pennsylvania, 1941), pp. 1-17.

12 F. H. Hilliard, *A Short History of Education in British West Africa* (London: Thomas Nelson and Sons Ltd., 1957), pp. 157-158.

13 R. J. Wingfield, 'The Saga of Lokoja's 100 Years—Features of the Northern Region of Nigeria' (Kaduna: Northern Nigeria Information Service, Baraka Press, May 1960), pp. 8-9.

14 Sonia F. Graham, *Government and Mission Education in Northern Nigeria 1900-1919,* (Ibadan University Press, 1966).

15 Ibid., p. 19.

16 Ibid.

17 Ibid., p. 7.

18 Ibid., pp. 11-12.

19 Ibid., pp. 13-14.

20 Ibid., p. 25.

21 Ibid., p. 26.

22 Ibid., p. 27.

23 Ibid., p. 32.

24 Ibid., p. 40.

25 Ibid., p. 42.

26 Ibid., pp. 46-48.

27 Ibid., p. 51.

28 Ibid.

29 Ibid., pp. 52-59.

30 L. J. Lewis, *Society, Schools and Progress in Nigeria* (Oxford: Pergamon Press, 1965), pp. 23-30.

31 W. R. S. Miller, *Reflections of a Pioneer* London: C.M.S., 1936), p. 93.

32 T. T. Solaru, *Teacher Training in Nigeria* (Ibadan University Press, 1964), p. 22.

2

THE ORDINANCES

THE failure of the 'Zaria Experiment' mentioned earlier, shifted the responsibility of providing education for the Muslims of Northern Nigeria to the colonial government. Hanns Vischer, a Swiss man who later became a British national provided this alternative. Hanns Vischer had first gone to Northern Nigeria as a missionary in Miller's party. He resigned after serving for two years to join the Imperial Service as Assistant Resident. On his appointment as the man to organize education for the Muslims of Northern Nigeria in 1908, he was given six months leave to study the education systems of Egypt, the Sudan, the Gold Coast (Ghana) and Lagos. He returned more favourably disposed to adopting the Sudan system which appeared to him to be achieving success because its methods had been so adapted to the requirements and the conditions of the country that education was becoming popular. [1]

On Vischer's return he proposed that the government schools should be confined to Muslim districts and that the missions be free to extend their work among the non-Muslims. Their schools should be subject to inspection by officials of the Education Department with a view to the eventual formation of a system of grants-in-aid. The extension of government schools to non-Muslim areas was to be considered after the successful establishment of Muslim schools. Thus Vischer was not only committed to displacing the Christian missions in Muslim districts but was also determined to compete with the missions in pagan areas at a later date.[2]

Meanwhile, the Resident of Sokoto started an unofficial school in 1909 and about the same time another school was started in Katsina by the Resident there. These were intended for the sons of Chiefs. Vischer recommended that these and others similarly established by other Residents should receive the government's recognition. The first government elementary school was planned for late 1910, to be followed a year later by a primary school in a central position. Kano was the site he suggested. Vischer's plans were not significantly different from Miller's ambitions. There was to be a class for the sons of Chiefs which began in March 1910 with 31 pupils. The teacher-training class began earlier in September 1909, preparatory to the opening of the elementary school in Kano in October 1910. The subjects taught were Hausa reading and writing in Roman script, hygiene, arithmetic up to simple decimals and fractions, and the geography of the Protectorate, Africa and the Empire. Local history and the history of the British Empire were to be added when textbooks became available. By December 1911, there were 80 in the Mallam's class, 102 pupils in the new elementary school, 97 in the school for the sons of Chiefs, 31 in the workshop and 10 in the surveying class.[3] This was tremendous progress for such a short time among people who were considered extremely suspicious of Western education. Vischer wrote in his report:

> The most encouraging part of the work is the natives' ready response to our efforts, and this fact, I think, justifies our highest hopes for the future. The arrival of *almajirai* (young mallam students) from outlying districts and the desire for schools expressed by the Emirs, indicate a real demand for further extension of our work.[4]

Vischer's appointment as Director of Education in 1910 marked the establishment of the Department of Education in the Protectorate of Northern Nigeria with its headquarters in Kano.[5]

Sir Frederick Lugard became Governor-General and Commander-in-Chief of the Colony and Protectorate of Nigeria on 1 January 1914. He was committed to the amalgamation of Northern and Southern Nigeria. Nigeria was therefore in the process of being unified and there was a strong possibility that administration would become more centralized. Lugard introduced to the South the system of Indirect Rule operating in the North, and also evolved an Education Ordinance in 1916 which was to reflect the unity of the whole country.[6]

THE EDUCATION ORDINANCE 1916

Before 1916

Education ordinances relating to Nigeria were passed in 1882 and 1887. In 1882, the Colony of Lagos was still united to the Gold Coast Colony (Ghana) and the first education ordinance was enacted to apply to the West African territories. Lagos Colony was the only part of Nigeria that was affected by this ordinance. Following the separation of Lagos Colony from Ghana and the establishment of the Colony and the Protectorate of Lagos, the first Nigerian education ordinance was enacted in 1887. The effect of this ordinance was, however, limited to Lagos Colony.[7]

The main features of these ordinances were: *(1)* they marked the beginning of a defined relationship between the missions and the government, *(2)* they provided for the setting up of a Board of Education and an official Inspector of Schools, and *(3)* they provided recurrent grants based on the system of 'payment by results', that is, on the ability of the pupils to pass examinations.[8]

Education Ordinance 1916

Lugard's opinion of the products of pre-1916 education in Southern Nigeria was very low indeed. He observed that a system that had already been proved faulty in India was being reproduced with disastrous results in Southern Nigeria. He maintained that such education produced discontent and unjustified assumptions of self-importance. He judged that while the rudiments of education were widespread, the result had been the decay of family and social discipline, discontent and hostility to authority.[9] Lugard, therefore, sought to build an education system which would promote 'a better standard of discipline, self control and integrity' combined with educational qualifications more adequate to the demands of the state and of commerce.

Principles embodied

Lugard himself summarized the principles embodied in the Code of 1916 as follows:

(1) That the primary object of all schools should be the formation of character and habits of discipline, rather

than the mere acquisition of a certain amount of book learning or technical skill, and that the grant-in-aid should be based in part on success in this direction.

(2) Teaching should be adapted to the needs of the pupils whether they are attending to qualify for clerical or other service; or, on the other hand, have no wish to leave their village and the pursuits which their fathers have followed.

(3) The proportions of teachers to pupils should be adequate, they should be properly qualified, and their ability improved. Adequate grants must be given to assisted schools (from which government and commercial clerks were drawn) to enable them to pay adequate salaries to their staff.

(4) That educational agencies whether controlled by government or by mission should co-operate with a common object; and as far as possible by similar methods of discipline and instruction.

(5) Continuation and evening classes for advanced and specialized study, and institutions and classes for the training of teachers, should receive special encouragement.

(6) The value of religion irrespective of creed or sect, and the sanction and incentive it affords, should be recognized and utilized as an agent for this purpose, together with secular moral instruction.

(7) Government should exercise some measure of control over all schools, even though not assisted by grants, and endeavour to bring them into line with the general policy.

(8) The schools should, as far as possible, be conducted in accordance with native customs in matters of dress and etiquette in order that pupils may not become denationalized or consider themselves a class apart.[10]

Draft Education Ordinance

Lugard first produced a draft education ordinance and draft code regulations for grants-in-aid to voluntary agency schools on his voyage home from Nigeria in April 1914.

Some of the innovations which the new ordinance planned to introduce were:

(1) A new approach to grants-in-aid. Up to this time payment of grants depended upon examination results conducted by government inspectors of education. The new code proposed that examination results should account for only 40 per cent of the assessment. 'Adequacy and efficiency of staff' were also to be taken into account in assessing grants.

(2) Re-organization of the school system. Three types of education were envisaged; literary, rural and technical.

(a) Literary education was to provide clerks and teachers. These would come from the provincial schools. The provincial school went up to Standard VII, and was situated at a provincial headquarters under a British headmaster. It was a boarding school giving special encouragement to games. Evening classes for the teaching of advanced subjects like agriculture and survey and a class for the training of teachers were to be held at the provincial school.[11]

(b) There was to be a rural school for peasants under an African schoolmaster. The curriculum was to include arts and crafts, practical agriculture, carpentry and smithing, hygiene, local geography, colloquial English (in the South), Hausa (in the North) and rudimentary arithmetic. The purpose of such a school was the training of character, discipline, industry and the improvement of the standard of life in the pupils' own villages.

(c) Technical education. The object was to improve the training often given in government workshops to illiterate men who could never become first-class workmen. Lugard insisted on a Standard IV or V qualification for entry in order to improve the status of the apprentice and the artisan so that they might be recognized as being of the same status as clerks. There was to be a close link between teacher training institutions and technical education.

(3) Board of Education. The ordinance provided for one Board of Education for the northern provinces and another for the colony and southern provinces. Each Board's duties were to be prescribed by the Governor.[12]

Reactions to the draft code

The code had been sent to Managers of assisted schools,

government inspectors and the Directors of Education for comments. The reception given to Lugard's suggestion in Southern Nigeria had been gratifying, and he had his draft amended by the Attorney-General to include some of the alterations suggested to him.

The main opposition to the 1916 Ordinance came from Northern Nigeria and the Colonial Office in London.[13]

Hanns Vischer, the Director of Education, was working in the War Office in London at this time and Mr. H.C. Brooks was Acting Director of Education for the northern provinces of Nigeria. Brook's comments on the draft code were as follows:

> With regard to the Draft Education Code, I have the honour to submit the following for consideration:
>
> *(1)* The code appears to me to be more suited to a more advanced stage of education than that at present attained by the schools in the Northern Provinces, while its aims as revealed by the stress laid upon the successful passing of the Cambridge Senior Local Examination are opposed to the spirit of the system in use here. It is still early in the development of our methods to be able definitely to state the needs of the country.
>
> *(2)* From a practical point of view the department will not be in a position to carry out the necessary examinations and inspections, at any rate in the near future, and at the same time carry out the duties already assigned to it.
>
> *(3)* The regulations governing the registration and promotion of the native teachers would not suit the conditions obtaining in the Northern Provinces and would bear hardly on many valuable teachers. Many of the present teachers and many others, who will in the future become teachers, will prove quite incapable of fulfilling the regulations regarding promotion and yet are admirable instructors in the subjects which they now teach and are fully fit for promotion in due course.
>
> *(4)* That the matter be submitted to the Director of Education, Northern Provinces (then at the War Office in London), for his views and that the Code remain in abeyance as far as the Northern Provinces are concerned.[14]

Contrary to the views that Vischer was never consulted,[15]

his letter from the War Office dated 11 December 1915, contained the following comments:

> With reference to the Draft Education Code and the letter from Mr. Brooks, I regret that I have not the time to state my opinion at any length. I fully endorse all Mr. Brooks says only I differ from him when he says that the Code appears to be more suited to a more advanced stage of education than at present attained by the schools in the Northern Provinces. These schools have been initiated and developed on lines altogether different and unless this will be altered and a different system introduced, this code cannot meet at any time the requirements of our schools.
>
> If our aim is a national system of education for the people in the Northern Provinces it seems to me dangerous to lay down any hard and fast rules as we have to feel our way very carefully in developing and perfecting our system. In my opinion we *are not* yet in a position to lay down detailed instructions or rules for the management of our schools, the training of our teachers, etc. Also I cannot see how the same Code can ever apply to the Southern and Northern Provinces.
>
> Finally I would call attention to the enormous amount of work lying before us with the preparation of school text books.
>
> Hanns Vischer (Signed) [16]

The comments from Brooks and Vischer really set the stage for the stiff battle Lugard had to fight with the Colonial Office in London over the Draft Education Ordinance of 1914. It was clear from these replies, however, that the educational development of Northern Nigeria was not only different but was calculated to be lower than that of the South. Vischer, the Director of Education, was positive that the same code could never apply to both the northern and southern provinces of Nigeria and that the northern teachers were quite incapable of fulfilling the academic requirements for promotion. Much as later events in the history of Nigeria proved Vischer wrong on both points, the Colonial Office nevertheless sided with him at this time.

The arguments put forward by Lugard against the points raised by the Colonial Office in connection with the Draft

Education Code 1914, demonstrate clearly the issues involved.[17] The first argument advanced by the Colonial Office was that grants to mission schools 'might involve the introduction of the Europeanized system of education which has tended to produce such unsatisfactory results in West Africa'. Lugard's argument against this point was that there already existed in the northern provinces a large and constantly increasing number of mission schools situated for the most part in the 'pagan' districts. Any proposal to discourage or if possible eliminate them was not likely to be effective or desirable. Besides, Lugard insisted that it was by means of the grant code itself and by co-operation between government and other agencies that the most effective check could be obtained against the evils which were feared. By recognition and by example, the government might be able to induce the acceptance of methods and principles even beyond those that were established by the code.[18]

Another point raised against the code pertained to the Board of Education. The Colonial Office held that a Board should exist to keep education and public opinion in touch, and since there was no public opinion on matters of education in the northern provinces, a Board would be superfluous and might interfere with Vischer's work. Lugard replied to say that the main object of the Board would be to facilitate co-operation between government and non-government educational agencies. Representatives on the Board would have the opportunity to ventilate and determine the problems of education with the goodwill and assistance of those who had daily experience of the practical work of education. The Governor, he went on, would take care to see that the powers of the Director of Education were not unduly decreased.[19]

For the Colonial Office to have maintained that at this time there was no public opinion on matters of education in the northern provinces was not only unfortunate but was also very unrealistic. If the experiment which Vischer was working at was to be truly indigenous then Nigerians themselves should have participated in the decision-making.

Another charge brought against Lugard's code was that it did not recognize that the southern and northern provinces presented 'essentially different problems'. Lugard's reply was that more than half the northern provinces were peopled by primitive pagan tribes whose education presented precisely the same problem as the corresponding tribes of the South. From the point of view of religion Lugard argued the South contained large numbers of Muslims; even in Lagos itself the population was half Muslim. Lugard then went on to affirm:

> I do not regard the Amalgamation which I was selected to carry out as a geographical, political or more especially as a financial expression. I regard it, as I know that you do, rather as a means whereby each part of Nigeria may be raised to the level of the highest plane attained by any particular part, and in the matter of education, each part has something to learn from the other.[20]

Despite these strong arguments put up by Lord Lugard, the reply from the Colonial Office merely confirmed that as far as the northern provinces were concerned the battle was a lost one. The reply was as follows:

> In view of the explanation which you have afforded, I am prepared to agree to your proposals so far as the Southern Provinces are concerned.
>
> As regards the Northern Provinces I am prepared in deference to your views, to agree to the establishment of a Board of Education. The functions of the Board should, however, be confined entirely to Christian and non-Government schools, and if a system of grants to Mission Schools is introduced it should be strictly limited to schools in the districts of Northern Nigeria where such schools are already established.
>
> I have etc.
> A. Bonar Law
> Downing Street
> 3rd January, 1916[21]

Effects of Colonial Office reactions to the draft code

With the passing of the 1916 Education Ordinance as amended by the Colonial Office, there was to be one education ordinance for the whole of Nigeria ('Colony and Protectorate: An Ordinance Relating to Education No.50 of 1916').

However, this did not result in the establishment of a unified Education Department and the Boards of Education for the northern and southern provinces were constituted differently as follows:[22]

Colony and Southern Provinces	*Northern Provinces*
The Lieutenant-Governor	The Lieutenant-Governor
The Administrator	A Resident to be nominated by the Governor
The Director of Education	The Director of Education
The Director of the Medical and Sanitary Service	Two other persons to be appointed by the Governor
Four other persons to be appointed by the Governor	

The Board for the northern provinces had only two non-official members, this reduction making a permanent official majority. Moreover the President of the Board, in normal circumstances the Lieutenant-Governor, had a casting vote as well as a member's vote. The quorum was the President plus three members. As there were only two unofficial members, it followed therefore that no situation could arise in which the officials could be outvoted, if they were in accord. This gave Vischer the protection he wanted as his work was completely insulated from public criticism and influence.[23]

Article 13e of the Education Ordinance was a direct quote from the Colonial Office:

> No grant shall be made to any school or training institution which is a Mission or other Christian school or training institution situated in a District of the Northern Provinces in which no Mission or other Christian school or training institution is established at the commencement of the Ordinance.[24]

This, in effect, meant that the missionary activities in the field of education were henceforth restricted. Bishop Tugwell was quick in his reaction to this particular clause of the ordinance. He wrote asking for an interview with the Lieutenant-Governor commenting on the clause as follows:

> It is not easy to discover what this means, unless it is the intention of the Government deliberately to exclude all such Christian schools or training institutions as may be established subsequently to the commencement of the Ordinance as grant-earning schools.[25]

Bishop Tugwell received a reply from the Office of the Lieutenant-Governor to say that, 'I am to add that the section in question was inserted at the direction of the Secretary of State for the Colonies'.[26] After receiving such a firm reply Bishop Tugwell could not press any further. It followed, therefore, that although the expansion of mission schools was not legally forbidden, this refusal of all state-aid was discouraging and demonstrated in unmistakable terms the opposition of administration to missionary expansion in the field of education.

Opposition to this particular clause (13e) continued to mount and in July 1917 the clause was dropped through a Nigeria *Gazette* notice of amendment. Following this amendment, the government published in August 1917 new regulations which tightened the government's control over mission schools in Northern Nigeria.[27]

In order to put whatever might be said about all education ordinances within the period of study 1916-1966 into proper perspective, it is important that we examine in some detail the first of these ordinances, Lugard's draft education ordinance.

The first part of the ordinance defined terms ranging from the word 'school' to 'Inspector'. These definitions attempted to identify the intentions and objectives of the government in applying the rules to particular situations. For example, allowance was made for 'Proprietors' to operate schools side by side with the government schools.

Section 3 particularly emphasized the powers given to the Governor for establishing government schools in Nigeria. This section underscored the government's prerogative in establishing schools.

Section 4 dealt with the constitution of the Boards of Education. This Board was crucial to the development of education throughout all the stages. The Board was supposed to make the government aware of public reactions to education. The composition of such Boards at each stage of educational development was truly indicative of how much lay participation the government was prepared to accommodate.

The 1916 Ordinance was very brief by comparison with the succeeding ordinances. The sections following Section 4 are gazette notices of the composition of different school committees set-up in the provinces. It is significant that both at board and committee levels, the administrators, not necessarily educationists, provided leadership in educational matters. This was in line with the colonial policy of making sure that school management did not outstrip administrative expediency. The functions of the boards and committees were therefore clearly defined by law in Sections 5-7.

It was in the interest of the government itself that the management of non-government schools should be controlled. Sections 8-10 indicated conditions for the appointment of school managers, returns to be furnished to the Governor by managers and the powers of the government to inspect all such schools.

Sections 11-14 dealt with the financing of schools through grants-in-aid. Conditions were stipulated by the government that non-government schools were supposed to meet before the government could assist in any way with finance. It was possible under certain conditions for the assistance to be withdrawn.

Sections 15-17 dealt with the exclusive powers of the Governor to close down non-government schools.

Section 18 dealt with regulations that the Governor-in-Council could make to give effect to the ordinance.*

GENERAL EFFECTS OF THE CODE

The following table clearly illustrates the educational development which took place between 1916 and 1926, the year in which a new ordinance came into being. In any comparison between the North and South at this time, it is important to

---

*The 1916 Education Ordinance is reproduced in the Appendix on pp. 91-98.

Growth of Primary Education[30]

Region	Year	GOVERNMENT AND NATIVE ADMINISTRATION				VOLUNTARY AGENCY (ASSISTED)				VOLUNTARY AGENCY (UNASSISTED).			
		No. of Schools	Average Attendance			No. of Schools	Average Attendance			No. of Schools	Average Attendance		
			Boys	Girls	Total		Boys	Girls	Total		Boys	Girls	Total
SOUTHERN PROVINCES AND LAGOS AND COLONY	1912	59	3,873	111	3,984	91	9,673	2,059	11,732	(a)	(a)	(a)	20,100
	1926	58	8,800	575	9,374	192	28,229	7,046	32,275	3,578	(a)	(a)	96,600
	1930	64	9,599	1,061	10,660	275	37,885	10,534	48,419	2,387	72,951	9,403	82,354
	1937	108	10,667	1,516	12,183	339	52,803	16,661	69,464	3,086	116,819	28,144	136,963
	1947 (c)	183	21,604	4,436	26,040 (c)	473	114.935	38,824	153,759 (c)	4,328	294,322	64,270	858,592 (d)
NORTHERN PROVINCES	1912	5	(a)	(a)	350	—	—	—	—	29	(a)	(a)	(a)
	1926	68	(a)	(a)	2,207	1	(a)	(a)	(a)	56	(a)	(a)	3,003
	1937	195	(a)	(a)	9,130	22	2,623	807	3,430	322	5,909	806	7,709
	1947 (c)	400 (b)	19,551	5,571	25,122 (c)	167	15,804	5,584	21,388 (c)	543	18,107	6,045	24,452

(a) Figures not known.

(b) Includes 12 Middle Schools giving a five-year course subsequent to a four-year Junior Primary Course.
Includes a number of pupils in one assisted voluntary agency school.

(c) The figures shown for 1947 are figures of enrolment, average attendance figures not being available, and are from returns made in respect of the year 1946.

(d) In addition, there was, in returns for the year 1946, record of 23,873 boys and 6,161 girls in private venture schools, in the southern provinces.

remember that the North was a late starter in the field of Western education. Besides, the North was affected more severely by the effect of the First World War as most of the teachers who were expatriates had to withdraw from the country. All the same the results reveal a considerable achievement.[28]

The total number of children in schools in the southern provinces in 1912 was 35,716 and this number increased to 138,248 by 1926. This was an increase of over 290 per cent. In 1912, the government schools provided only 8½ per cent of the total number of children while in 1926 the percentage fell to 6½ per cent.[29]

In the northern provinces there were only 954 children in school in 1912 as compared with 35,716 in the South. By 1926 the children in the northern schools increased to 5,210 as compared with 138,248 in the South. The increase of over 400 per cent for the northern provinces was phenomenal. This impressive growth emphasized the potentials and possibilities that were available. But when one remembers that the population of the North was almost 1½ times as great as the South, the wide gap between the North and the South appears very serious.[30] Mr. F. Urling Smith, Director of Education Northern Provinces, 1926-1929, commented on the situation as follows:

> There's now a tide running in the affairs of the Northern Provinces. How long an opportunity of taking it at the flood is hardly possible to say; but that we are missing some of it I have no doubt.[31]

The situation immediately after the First World War was summed up in the following words by Sir Hugh Clifford, the Governor:

> In the Northern Provinces there has been until recently a certain tendency to regard education of the local population with some uneasiness and suspicion, as a process likely to exert a disintegrating and demoralizing effect upon the character of those who are subjected to it; and where this feeling has been overcome, a further tendency is observable to regard education too exclusively as a handmaid of

> administration . . . . After two decades of British occupation, the Northern Provinces have not yet produced a single native . . . who is sufficiently educated to enable him to fill the most minor clerical post in the office of any government department . . . . The African staff of these offices throughout the Northern Provinces are therefore manned by men from the Gold Coast, Sierra Leone and from the Southern Provinces of Nigeria . . . . Education in the North has been practically confined to the vernacular and to Arabic, has been allowed to become the almost exclusive prerequisite of the children of the local ruling classes, and has for its main object the equipment of these children with just sufficient knowledge of reading, writing and arithmetic to enable them in after life to fill posts in one or another of the various Native Administrations. . . .[32]

This critical observation of the educational system in the North could not have come from a better person than the Governor himself. His point of view was later reinforced by T.T. Solaru of Oxford University Press, Ibadan, when he said:

> In the North, Government experiment at making education practical had not in twenty years, succeeded in producing northerners capable of filling minor government posts. In trying to encourage the local languages to the exclusion of English in the lower schools, difficulties arose which made it impossible to expand the scope and extent of teacher training.[33]

It could be deduced, therefore, that Vischer's educational experiment in the North which the 1916 Ordinance completely approved and protected, did not out work entirely in the interests of the people since *(1)* it failed to take account of the needs of the locality in particular and the country in general, (the impact of the railway and the expanding mercantile and governmental operations required trained local personnel for clerical and artisan posts which Vischer's system refused to acknowledge), *(2)* the educational system which was declared to be truly indigenous in character included in its primary curriculum subjects like the history and geography of the British Empire, *(3)* where agriculture was taught, particular attention was paid to cultivation of crops which might form the staples for exports,[34] and *(4)* to have insisted on the extensive use of the native languages under such difficult conditions—lack of textbooks and native teachers, numerous languages and dialects—was to have deliberately adopted the slow process. Miller's remarks are pertinent here:

> All this might have been foreseen and prevented. The foolish policy which withheld the study of the English language during the earlier stages of education and development of the Northern Province has brought a sad Nemesis upon the people themselves. Many years ago, I pleaded for full instruction in English, not only as a subject, but as the vehicle of instruction, realizing that English must certainly become the language both of literature and of commerce of the near future. It was in vain.[35]

He went on to say that the policy of preserving the culture of the North was overdone and that the government policy was dictated by political considerations rather than by the educational needs of the people.[36]

For Vischer to have insisted on teaching the people their own culture to the exclusion of all other cultures through schools of Western origin was not only presumptuous but was to attempt the near impossible. It was Murray who once said of the Nigerian student:

> We foreigners cannot give him African culture, because it is not ours to give. We can only give him European culture, because that is what we have . . . But the African heritage includes all that has ever taken place since the world began, if only it can be put at his disposal.[37]

The 1916 Education Ordinance encouraged educational expansion in the South while it limited missionary expansion in the North, and by approving and protecting Vischer's educational experiment the ordinance slowed down comparatively the educational development in the North. Vischer's experiment emphasized liberal education to the neglect of relevant vocational training that was badly needed at this time. This led to the influx into Northern Nigeria of people from the South to occupy important civil service posts, and this in turn led to suspicion and bitter resentment and so paved the way for the Nigerian Civil War.[38]

THE EDUCATION ORDINANCE 1926

Background and principles embodied

The dominant feature of the years immediately following the First World War was the rapid increase in the number of unassisted schools, especially in the southern part of Nigeria. The schools had multiplied so rapidly as to be beyond the effective supervision and control of many of the agencies which had sponsored them in answer to local demands, and they were quite beyond the control of the Education Department. The concern aroused in the Governor's (Sir Hugh Clifford) mind by this state of affairs found ultimate expression in an important memorandum which he prepared in 1925 for the Secretary of State's Advisory Committee on Native Education in British Tropical Africa.[39]

The memorandum recognized without reservation the need for the government of Nigeria to spend a very much larger sum on education than had been spent in the past. That the government did not exercise supervision or control over the bulk of educational activities in the southern provinces was another point that was emphasized in the memorandum. Sir Hugh Clifford referred to some schools in the southern provinces as 'hedge schools' and insisted that the control of these schools was the 'crux of the problem'. He argued that the products of the 'system or lack of system' were cut adrift from their fellows and from their tribal and family obligations. He held the view that it was government's business to provide a solution for an 'utterly deplorable state of affairs'.[40]

It may well be that the memorandum expressed rather exaggerated alarm at the unsatisfactory by-products of a process which was in certain respects a healthy and vigorous social phenomenon—and which in any case was the inevitable result of the forces affecting the community at that time that were not entirely susceptible to official control. Be that as it may, the fact remains that small schools had multiplied fast in the South and from lack of proper supervision and shortage of qualified teachers many of the schools were of very poor quality.[41]

Sir Hugh Clifford sought to secure control of educational expansion by conferring on a representative Board of Education executive powers to regulate the opening of new schools and to close any schools which might be proved to be inadequately equipped, housed or managed, or in which the teachers were themselves too ignorant to be able to impart education of a really sound character. He also proposed that in future, elementary education should be exclusively entrusted in the southern provinces to the Christian missions. This proposal marked the first definite departure from the policy followed previously of direct government intervention through the provision of government elementary schools.[42]

Innovations

As a result of Sir Hugh Clifford's recommendations, a new education ordinance came into force on 26 May 1926. This was aimed primarily at the condition of schools in the southern provinces. For all practical purposes, the 1926 Education Ordinance (No. 14 of 1926) for the northern provinces incorporated most of the provisions of the Education Ordinance of 1916. The new features of the new ordinance were:[43]

(a) Definitions

1916	*1926*
'School' means an institution in which more than ten pupils are systematically taught, and in which any person is engaged to impart education.	'School' means an institution in which not less than ten pupils receive regular instruction and includes any assembly of not less than ten pupils for the purpose of receiving regular instructions, and any institution for the training of teachers.

(b) Composition of the Board of Education

In the 1916 Ordinance, only two non-official people were to

serve on the Board. This was increased to four in the 1926 Ordinance to make it similar to the situation in the southern provinces in 1916.

These were the only changes. They were significant in the sense that the new definition of 'School' not only improved upon that of 1916 but enlarged the idea of a school to include a teacher training institution and 'any assembly of not less than ten pupils'. The latter clause was rather ambiguous as it could also refer to any religious assembly. This was later dropped. By increasing the non-official representation on the Board of Education to four, there was more opportunity for obtaining public opinion than before.[44]

On 17 July 1929, the Education Departments of the northern and southern provinces were united under the directorship of Mr. E.R.J. Hussey. He formulated a policy calculated to improve the quality and quantity of education in Nigeria. Mr. Hussey's policy was designed to correct the orientation towards the Standard VI examination which was given so much emphasis by the Education Code. He accordingly proposed the introduction in the southern provinces of a six-year primary school system. Beginning with the three Rs, teaching would be in the vernacular (where English was not the lingua franca). Agriculture in rural areas and handicrafts in towns were to be special features of the curriculum. English would be taught as a language from the third year of the elementary school.[45]

To achieve this, the curriculum of teacher training institutions should correlate with the activities of daily life. It was obvious that such training was not being done in the existing higher elementary colleges. Hussey, therefore, proposed the setting up of elementary centres by the government. For the northern provinces, three government elementary centres for vernacular teachers were to be established which would give a three-year course in general education and proficiency in teaching the elementary school syllabus. The medium of instruction was to be Hausa. Meanwhile local teacher training classes for supplying village assistant schoolmasters were to continue until the supply of better trained teachers could catch up with the demand. All these centres would be under the care of superintendents of education assisted by experienced elementary teachers from England. The syllabus was to include practical agriculture and handicrafts.[46]

General effects of the Ordinance

The Education Ordinance of 1926 aimed at providing a better quality of education through *(1)* increased direct government control and supervision, *(2)* co-operation with voluntary agencies by means of increased subsidies to schools and training institutions, and *(3)* by an attempt to improve the quality and status of teachers. That it did not succeed to any great extent was partly due to the great slump in international trade.

Its positive effect was particularly felt in the pagan areas of the North. For in 1926 there were only a little over 5,000 primary school enrollees but by 1947 the enrolment had climbed to approximately 71,000.

The group that benefitted most from the new government policy in addition to the new enrollees who could find places, were the teachers in the mission schools, since the greater part of the grants-in-aid went to pay the salaries of qualified instructors.

In addition, the government began to stress quality and the need for better qualified teachers, with the result that it raised the standards for teacher qualification.[47]

NOTES

1 Sonia F. Graham, *Government and Mission Education in Northern Nigeria 1900-1919* (Ibadan University Press, 1966), pp. 58-71.

2 Ibid., p. 75.

3 Ibid., pp. 79-85.

4 Ibid., p. 86.

5 D. H. Williams, *A Short Survey of Education in Northern Nigeria* (Kaduna: Ministry of Education, Northern Region, 1959), p. 7.

6 Government Printer, 'Annual Report of the Department of Education—1st April 1951 to 31st March 1952' (Lagos, Nigeria: Government Printer, 1954), p. 7.

7 Ibid., p. 6.

8 F. H. Hilliard, *A Short History of Education in British West Africa* (London: Thomas Nelson and Sons Ltd., 1956) pp. 122-123.

9 Solaru, op. cit., p. 23.

10 Ibid., pp. 23-25.

11 Ibid., pp. 25-26.

12 Ibid., pp. 26-27.

13 Graham, op. cit., p. 133.

14 Confidential No. 1279/1915—National Archives, Kaduna.

15 Graham, op. cit., p. 138.

16 Director of Education N.P., S.N.P. 9C. 119/1915, War Office, Whitehall, December 11, 1915, Archives, Kaduna.

17 Lord Lugard: SNP8 File No.87/1917, Archives Kaduna. (Extracts from F. D. Lugard Governor-General's letter to the Right Honourable A. Bonar Law P.C., M.P. Secretary of State for the Colonies, written in London dated 14th August 1915.)

18 Ibid.

19 Ibid.

20 Ibid.

21 Bonar A. Law, 'A reply to Lord Lugard's extracts' (Kaduna: Archives, Downing Street, January 3, 1916).

22 Colony and Protectorate, *An Ordinance Relating to Education* (December, 1916), p. 2.

23 Graham, op. cit., p. 139.

24 The Education Ordinance 1916, No. 50 of 1916.

25 H. Tugwell, 'Letter from Bishop Tugwell, Lokoja, Nigeria, October 30, 1916' (Kaduna: Archives).

26 Secretary, Northern Provinces, 'Reply to Bishop Tugwell' File No. SNP8/4, 46/7; SM1002/1916, Lokoja (Kaduna: Archives).

27 Graham, op. cit., pp. 144-145.

28 S. Phillipson, *Grants-In-Aid of Education in Nigeria* (Government Printer, Lagos, 1948), p. 106.

29 Ibid.

30 Ibid.

31 Solaru, op. cit., p. 46.

32 Reginald Bunting, *The Educated African* (New York: Frederick A. Praeger, 1962), p. 365.

33 Solaru, op. cit., p. 73.

34 Graham, op. cit., p. 80.

35 W. Miller, *Have We Failed in Nigeria?* (Lutterworth Press, 1947), pp. 12-25.

36 Ibid.

37 A. Victor Murray, *The School in the Bush* (London: Longman, Green and Company, 1929), p. 329.

38 Auberon Waugh and Suzanne Cronje, *Biafra: Britain's Shame* (London: Michael Joseph, 1969), pp. 19-20.

39 S.C.M.G. Phillipson, *Grants in Aid of Education in Nigeria. A Review with Recommendations* (Lagos: Government Printer, 1948), pp. 17-18.

40 Ibid., p. 18.

41 Ibid.

42 Ibid.

43 Ordinance, No. 50 of 1916—An Ordinance Relating to Education, and Ordinances No. 14 of 1926—An Ordinance Relating to Education in the Northern provinces.

44 Graham, op. cit., pp. 137-139.

45 Solaru, op. cit., pp. 48-49.

46 Ibid., p. 50.

47 Albert A. Blum, *Teacher Unions and Associations. A Comparative Study* (Urbana, Chicago: University of Illinois Press, 1970), p. 240.

3

EDUCATIONAL DEVELOPMENT 1929-55

THE Education Departments of Northern and Southern Nigeria were amalgamated in 1929. In that year there were 116 schools controlled by the government with the financial help of the native administrations. There were ninety-five elementary schools, eight craft schools, twelve primary (or middle) schools, and one secondary school. The total average attendance was 3,549 pupils.[1] The missions had 152 schools out of which only five were assisted.[2]

During the 'thirties' the elementary and middle schools of the North which have been described as government schools became more appropriately known as 'native administration schools'. By 1938 the number of these schools grew to 216 and there were ten middle schools working up to Class IV. The only full secondary school in the North was still controlled by the government. The voluntary agency schools numbered 383, more than doubling their number since 1929. They now received more financial assistance from the government than previously.[3]

The period 1926-1929 was one of relative financial prosperity during which the new ordinance operated without hindrance and educational progress was marked. However, due to the great slump in international trade a financial crisis developed and the 'thirties' were a period of setbacks and frustrations. The severe restrictions which financial exigencies placed on the scope and scale of government assistance throughout the decade had an adverse effect on the efficiency of the schools. The situation became so grave that by 1940 an application was made to the Secretary of State for the Colonies for a grant from the Parliamentary Vote for Colonial Development and Welfare with which the salaries of mission teachers could be improved. The Secretary of State was of the view that unless the Governor could produce plans for controlling educational expansion in Nigeria, such an application could not be considered.[4]

Accordingly, a plan covering a ten-year period was drawn up and submitted to the Secretary of State in 1942. The plan was, however, criticized as being inadequate and was rejected. One of the aims set out in the abortive plan was the provision of more adequate financial assistance to missions and other voluntary agencies. In order to achieve this, it was suggested that grants-in-aid be assessed at 100 per cent of the salaries of all certified teachers and special register teachers, and a maximum quota for each grade of teachers was laid down for each type of institution. The effect of this would have been to abolish the distinction between assisted and unassisted schools. The proposal was incorporated in a new education ordinance passed in 1942 which was designed to supersede that of 1926 and abolish the arrangement whereby education in the northern and southern provinces had been administered under different ordinances. The new ordinance was never brought into operation as the new basis for grant assessment did not receive the approval of the Secretary of State.[5]

As the financial situation had improved substantially by 1941, the government endeavoured to provide from its resources the funds necessary to pay adequate salaries to voluntary agency teachers. Thereafter, until 1948, interim measures were adopted by the government to pay voluntary agency teachers salaries commensurate with those of other salaried people of similar attainment.[6]

In 1944 the Director of Education undertook a review of educational policy with reference to the issues raised by the non-acceptance of recommendations contained in the Ten-Year Plan. After full consultation, a comprehensive memorandum on policy was drawn up in 1945. A plan, based on the memorandum, was formulated known as a Ten-Year Plan of Educational Development and this formed the subject of an application for assistance under the Colonial Development and Welfare Act. The major provisions of the plan were *(1)* extension of facilities for secondary education and teacher training, *(2)* the establishment of rural education centres, *(3)* the development of technical education, and

(4) a supplementary five-year plan under which the northern provinces would receive an additional £500,000 for the development of secondary, teacher training and senior primary education. The plan was substantially approved. It was necessary that a new education ordinance should be drafted to put the recommendations into effect.[7]

Before a new ordinance could be drafted, it also became necessary to review the process of assessing grants-in-aid and early in 1948 an investigation was undertaken by Mr. Phillipson (now Sir Sydney), with a view to making recommendations regarding the financial provisions of the ordinance. The results of his inquiry were published in a report, 'Grants-in-Aid of Education in Nigeria—A Review with Recommendations'. Following the publication of the report, a new ordinance was enacted in 1948 which together with the regulations came into effect on 1 January 1949.[8]

THE EDUCATION ORDINANCE 1948

Background and principles embodied

A bill entitled, 'An Ordinance to make better provision in regard to Education in Nigeria', was debated in the Regional Houses and thereafter in the Legislative Council before being assented to by the Governor in His Majesty's name on 10 September 1948. During the debate in the Northern Regional House of Assembly, the Regional Deputy Director of Education moving the motion of acceptance of the bill, introduced the bill by drawing the House's attention to the fact that *(1)* the bill was the first that would be valid throughout Nigeria, *(2)* it was framed with the avowed policy of giving members of the community an opportunity of expressing public opinion through membership of the various boards. He then went on to say:

> . . . since the Ordinance will cover the whole country and since there is, at present, very much greater educational activity in the East and West than in the North, it was inevitable that it should have what one might call a Southern flavour, and that procedure hitherto peculiar to the North should disappear. Certain sections may, there-

> fore, seem strange at first, but since we are trying to bring practice into line with that of the South we must also adopt procedure . . . By this Ordinance and the Regulations, the Northern Provinces will receive equal treatment with the East and West and I make a very serious appeal to the North to take advantage of it.[9]

The Provincial Member for Adamawa, the late Honourable Alhaji M. Muhammadu Ribadu did not appear to share the views of the Deputy Director with regard to the southern flavour of the bill when he said:

> Mr. President, Sir, formerly there were different Ordinances and syllabuses for the North and South. I believe that that was why the standard of education in the South was always higher than that of the North. Now it is a great advantage to the North to have one uniform Education Ordinance for the whole of Nigeria. The system of Grants-in-Aid has been reorganized on a better basis than before. The Native Administrations and Voluntary Agencies are now enabled to expand and improve the conditions of their schools and also employ more efficient teachers. It also enables the Government to have control over such schools . . . I support the Bill in principle.[10]

Generally, the reaction of the people to the 1948 Ordinance was a favourable one.

Innovations

The ordinance provided for the supersession of the old Colony and Southern Provinces Board of Education by a Central Board of Education and four Regional Boards. It thus introduced the regionalization of education by establishing three regional Deputy Directors of Education with Regional Boards. It further provided for the establishment of Local Education Committees and Local Education Authorities.[11]

Under the new ordinance no new school could be established without the consent of the appropriate Regional Deputy Director of Education. The Regional Deputy Director of Education could prohibit the opening of a new school if he was not satisfied that the school would be conducted efficiently or staffed adequately. An appeal from his decision could be made to the Regional Board of Education and thence, if necessary, to the Central Board of Education.[12]

The new grants-in-aid regulations provided for the award of assistance to all schools considered to be socially useful and efficient. Thus the voluntary agencies and the native administrations were given parity in grants-in-aid of education.[13]

The system hitherto in force for the granting of assistance from government funds to the schools of the voluntary agencies was completely revised. Specific conditions were laid down regarding the staffing arrangements, premises, equipment and management of a school; these had to be fulfilled if a school was to be eligible for a grant.[14]

The amount of financial assistance that could be paid to a qualified school was to be calculated in accordance with a fixed formula, consisting of the recognized expenses, namely the amount of the teachers' salaries together with a contribution. An assumed local contribution was assessed according to the stage of development of the area concerned.[15]

The new regulations therefore gave a logical basis of control over the development of the educational system by providing a set of criteria by which assistance to voluntary agency schools was to be determined. At the same time, the new regulations made it possible for the voluntary agencies to assess in advance the commitments which they and the community would incur.[16]

The first five years of the Ten-Year Development Plan came to an end in 1950-51 and during that year a revision of the Plan was made to cover the period 1951-56. The main effect of the revision was to reduce slightly the provision for development of general education in the eastern and western provinces, to provide the voluntary agencies with additional facilities for secondary education and teacher training in the northern provinces, and to increase considerably the provision for technical education throughout Nigeria.[17]

With the introduction of the new constitution, extensive amendments became necessary to the Education Ordinance (No.39/1948), to the Grants-in-Aid Regulations and to the

Education Regulations, 1949. The amendments required were so numerous that it was considered convenient to draft a new ordinance and new regulations so that the amended legislation might be available in as convenient a form as possible to those who would have to refer to it. Regulation No.17 of 1949 as amended became the Education (General) Regulations and for purposes of convenience formed schedule B to the new ordinance.[18]

The opportunity was taken to include in the new ordinance legislation enacted in 1950 and 1951 and also certain amendments which were recommended by the Central Board of Education at its meeting in 1951.[19]

The essential object of the ordinance was to bring legislation into line with the requirements of the new constitution. To that end, the membership of the Central and Regional Boards was changed slightly and the Colony Board was abolished with the inclusion of the Colony in the Western Region. As regards the grants-in-aid regulations, Regulation 2 was deleted since the payment of grants to the regions was governed by Section II of the Nigeria (Revenue Allocation) Order-in-Council, 1951. The new Regulation 16 provided for the revision of the rates of recognized expenses and assumed local contributions during 1952 for the three years from 1 January 1953.[20]

General effects of the Ordinance and Regulations

The Ten-Year Development Plan for Nigeria was revised and its items regionalized.[21]

The shortage of trained teachers rather limited expansion in the Northern Region as some native authorities could not open projected schools. This can be traced to the fact that a large number of teachers were engaged in political activities with the result that their services were lost for considerable periods each year.[22]

Junior secondary schools emerged to replace the middle schools in the North.

The first appeal in the Northern Region under Section 21 of the Education Ordinance 1952 was heard against the witholding of consent to open a Sudan Interior Mission

School at Matazu in Katsina Province. The appeal was heard by the reconstituted Northern Regional Board of Education. It was successful; a question of principle being involved (the right of a Christian community to establish its own school in a Muslim area where existing educational facilities were still inadequate to meet the needs of all children of school-going age). It is significant to note that the official members abstained from voting.[23]

Native authorities could invoke a Compulsory Attendance Order, if they wished and in certain areas this was done. There were cases where compulsory recruitment was directed mainly against the peasant class, and the children of the officials and more prosperous classes were left out. In the more backward areas, it was alleged that the power to invoke this order discriminated unfairly against the voluntary agencies.[24]

In many areas, the new salary scales hit the voluntary agency unassisted schools very hard. While it was not compulsory to pay the approved rates in unassisted schools, it was obviously undesirable to have teachers with similar qualifications on different rates, depending on whether they were working in an assisted or unassisted school.[25]

There were three salary scales operating in the Northern Region; government, native authority and voluntary agency scales. All were very similar, but there were slight differences so that it was possible for two teachers with the same seniority and the same qualifications working in adjacent schools to be paid at different rates. The differences were usually very small and sometimes the man who started on a lower salary finished on a higher one, or received more advantageous increments. This gave rise to dissatisfaction.[26]

Regulations were at last printed and made available for issue by managers to schools which could then for the first time comply with the regulation which required all assisted schools to be in possession of a copy of the ordinance.[27]

Comparative figures for primary education over the previous five years were as follows:

	Schools		*Pupils*	
	N.A.	V.A.	N.A.	V.A.
1949	532	851	33,510	62,088
1950	605	851	40,705	68,030
1951	646	889	41,891	65,670
1952	703	990	47,853	74,292
1953	744	1,033	51,303	92,506

These figures indicate that whereas in 1949 only one child in twenty-six was in school, four years later one in every seventeen was receiving some form of primary education. There were half as many more children in school than there were five years before. In 1952, 549 native administration primary schools were assisted and 154 unassisted; 614 voluntary agency schools were assisted and 365 unassisted. The voluntary agencies still seemed to be shouldering the greatest responsibility for education.[28]

EFFECTS OF CONSTITUTIONAL CHANGES

During 1954-55, the constitutional changes which followed the London Conference of August 1953, and its resumed meeting in Lagos in January 1954, became law on 1 October 1954. As a result of the new instruments of government the Education Department in the Northern Region was separated both from the central headquarters in Lagos and from the departments in the other regions in the federation. The Central Ministry of Education disappeared, and with it the Central Board of Education; the former office of the Inspector General of Education in Lagos was abolished, and the education service in the region became a part of the separate Northern Region Public Service. Various administrative links with the centre, such as those concerned with promotions, appointments, the certification of teachers, the control of examinations, and particularly the legislative controls contained in the Nigerian Education Ordinance of

1952, were finally severed to meet the circumstances of the new federation.[29]

The Education Department thus found itself in much the same position as it was in 1929, immediately before the appointment of the first Director of Education for Nigeria. There was one salient difference, however, which did not exist twenty-five years before. This was that the activities of the department were the sole responsibility of the Minister of Education in the regional government, and supervision of these activities was exercised on his behalf by the Permanent Secretary to the Ministry of Education.

With the introduction of the Federal Constitution in October 1954, an adapted education law was enacted in order to enable the ordinance of 1952 and its regulations to remain in force, *mutatis mutandis*.

THE EDUCATION ORDINANCE 1956

In 1956 the Northern Regional Legislature passed into law the new education ordinance, which superseded the 1952 ordinance previously applicable to the whole of Nigeria. A new Board of Education was constituted and provision for local education committees and advisory boards was made. Grants-in-aid for both capital and recurrent expenses were regularized and made available on equal terms to both native authorities and voluntary agencies.[31]

Innovations and general effects of the 1956 Education Ordinance

In November, the Ministry of Education in common with the other ministries in the Northern Region, was reorganized in connection with a process known as 'Integration'. This was done in fulfilment of Section 121 of the Nigeria (Constitution) Order-in-Council, 1954. As a result of 'Integration' the Department of Education, which had existed in the North since 1910, ceased to exist and was merged within the Ministry of Education. The offices of the Director and Deputy Director also ceased to exist and the holders of these two offices were appointed respectively as Adviser and Chief Inspector of Education, the latter assuming charge of the newly formed Inspectorate Division of the Ministry. The executive control of the ministry passed to the Permanent Secretary who was assisted by a deputy. The holders of these offices were administrative officers.[32]

The difference between the educational development of the riverain provinces of Northern Nigeria and that of the 'Far Northern' Provinces began to be more noticed and emphasized. Honourable Aliyu Makaman Bida, Minister of Education, in his preface to the Annual Report of 1954-55, made the following pertinent remarks:

> In my Preface to last year's Annual Report, I discussed the disquieting difference in educational demand as between the Riverain and the 'Far Northern' Provinces within the Region. It is my duty once more to invite the public's attention to the danger of uneven development which is likely to be caused by this difference . . .
>
> A Region in which some citizens thirst for 'Western' knowledge and others show little or no interest in it manifestly sets the Regional Government extremely difficult problems to solve.[33]

A new seven-year primary school syllabus was introduced in January 1956. This comprised a four-year primary and a three-year senior primary course, and replaced the former four-year primary followed by three-year middle school syllabus previously in use in the region and the 'southern' eight-year syllabus which was used by some of the voluntary agencies.[34]

With the general increase in the number of schools it became glaringly noticeable that no fees were paid in the schools, generally secondary schools, owned by government nor were they paid in a great number of native authority schools. Fees were collected in all voluntary agency schools and training centres and the more popular the schools were the easier it was to charge economic fees.

NOTES

1 Government Printer, Annual Report of the Department of Education 1st April, 1951 to 31st March, 1952. (Lagos, Nigeria: Government Printer, 1954), p. 12.

2 Ibid.

3 Ibid.

4 Ibid.

5 Ibid., p. 13.

6 Ibid.

7 Ibid., pp. 13-14.

8 Ibid.

9 Government Printer, *Northern Regional Council House of Assembly Debates, Second Series 15th, 16th and 17th July, 1948* (Kaduna), pp. 33-39.

10 Ibid., pp. 43-44.

11 Annual Reports, 1952, op. cit., p. 14.

12 Ibid., pp. 14-15.

13 Gary L. Cowan, James O'Connell, and David G. Scanlon, *Education and Nation-Building in Africa* (New York: Frederick A. Praeger, Publishers, 1965), pp. 78-119.

14 Ibid.

15 Ibid.

16 Ibid.

17 Government Printer, *Annual Report of the Department of Education, April, 1951-March 1952* (Lagos, Nigeria: Government Printer, 1954), p. 15.

18 Ibid., p. 27.

19 Ibid.

20 Ibid.

21 Solaru, op. cit., p. 99.

22 Government Printer, *Annual Report of the Education Department, Northern Region, April 1952-March 1953* (Lagos, Nigeria: Government Printer, 1954), pp. 8-24.

23 Ibid.

24 Ibid.

25 Government Printer, *Annual Report of the Education Department Northern Region, April 1953-March 1954* (Zaria, Nigeria: Gaskiya Corporation, 1954), pp. 14-19.

26 Ibid.

27 Ibid.

28 Ibid.

29 Government Printer, *Annual Report of the Education Department of the Northern Region of Nigeria, 1954-55* (Kaduna: Government Printer, 1956), p. 1.

30 Ibid., p. 12.

31 Williams, op. cit., p. 55.

32 Government Printer, *Annual Summary of the Education Department of the Northern Region of Nigeria* (Kaduna: Government Printer, 1959), p. 1.

33 Annual Report, 1954-55, op. cit., p. i.

34 Ibid., p. 8.

4

EDUCATIONAL DEVELOPMENT 1956-66

THE ASHBY REPORT

THE expansion of education in Northern Nigeria during this period was based mainly on targets given in the Ashby Report. In 1959, the Federal Government of Nigeria appointed a Commission, comprising Nigerian, American and British members, under the Chairmanship of Sir Eric Ashby, Master of Clare College, Cambridge, to 'conduct an investigation into Nigeria's needs in the field of Post-School Certificate and Higher Education over the next twenty years'. The commission met on three occasions and according to their report:

> We were fortunate to secure the services of five experts who prepared papers on aspects of our work. Professor F. Harbison, from Princeton University, prepared for us an estimate of manpower needs. . . . Mr. V.L. Griffiths, from Oxford University, prepared a report on teacher training, and Mr. M.W. Pritchard, one of Her Majesty's Inspectors of Schools prepared a report on Secondary schools. All three of these advisers spent some weeks in Nigeria on our behalf. . . .[1]

The commission's report ably set out the needs for developing education in Nigeria and the special needs of the Northern Region were fully recognized. The targets for the North as set out by the commission were *(1)* 25 per cent of all children to complete primary education, *(2)* 10 per cent of all children completing primary schooling to go to secondary education, and *(3)* 30 per cent of those completing the school certificate course to go for higher training, including degree courses at university.[2]

The government of Northern Nigeria quickly followed up this recommendation with a summary report on education in the region. The government set out its intention to encourage more even expansion of the educational facilities throughout the region. The two main objectives specifically stated were, the development of full seven year co-educational primary schools and the raising of the standards of such schools.[3]

THE OLDMAN REPORT

The increase in pupil enrolment which the government anticipated would follow the implementation of Ashby's recommendations and the administrative and financial commitments that would be required to prosecute successfully the educational programmes especially at the primary level led the government of the Northern Region in 1961 to invite Mr. H. Oldman, Chief Education Officer for the city of York in England, to undertake an inquiry and to write a report on the problems of administration and finance associated with the development of primary education. The following terms of reference were approved by the Executive Council:

(a) To advise on the form which the local contribution to the cost of Primary Education should take.

(b) To advise on whether there would be advantages in delegating control of primary education to Local Education Authorities and on whether or not such Local Education Authorities should have powers of precept.

(c) To advise on whether the English system of 'aided' and 'controlled' schools, or the Scottish system of transferred schools, or some modification of either would have relevance to Northern Nigerian conditions.

(d) To advise on any amendments to the Education Law and to the Grants-in-Aid Regulations that might be desirable.

(e) To advise on the future development of the Primary Schools' Inspectorate and on the administrative machinery required by Universal Primary Education.[4]

The Oldman Report recommended the formation of local education authorities, each with an education committee, and the training of suitably qualified officers to serve the new authorities. Provincial education secretaries were to be trained also and appointed so that they could help native authorities in the task of setting up the local education authorities.[5]

THE EDUCATION ORDINANCE 1962

The Education Law (No.17 of 1956) underwent an extensive review and the various changes and modifications based on Oldman's recommendations resulted in the new Education Law (N.N.No.43 of 1962). In 1964 the Education Law 1962 and the Education (Amendment) Law, 1963, were revised and appeared as Chapter 36 of the Laws of Northern Nigeria.[6]

Innovations and general effects of Education Ordinance 1962

The powers of the Minister of Education were clearly stated in the light of the powers conferred by the Constitution.[7] There were significant changes both in the ministry and in the provinces. The Chief Education Officer (General) became Senior Inspector Primary Schools and a post of Deputy Senior Inspector Primary Schools was created. In the provinces, the posts of Area Inspectors were abolished, together with the posts of Provincial Education Officers. The duties of Provincial Education Officers were divided into two: Inspection and Administration. The posts of Provincial Inspectors of Education and Provincial Education Secretaries were created. The former were to carry out the inspection and deal with professional matters and the latter were to deal with administration of schools.[8]

Forty-six local education authorities were set up and a further eight were to be set up in 1968. In the authorities' areas, voluntary agency primary schools were transferred to the authority concerned. The voluntary agencies retained the right to inspect religious teaching, which had to conform to that customarily given in school, and to approve the names of teachers proposed for engagement in their schools. The formation of the authorities led to considerable savings in administrative costs and a much closer control over these costs.[9]

A course for educational administrators was established at

the Institute of Administration, Zaria (now transferred to the Institute of Education, Zaria). The course trains education officers for local education authorities and also for government service in the ministry's headquarters and in provincial education offices.

The system of grant-aiding primary education was changed. Instead of being based on teachers' salaries plus additions for recognized expenses, less a sum assumed to be the local contribution, grants were now to be paid on a *per capita* basis on the number of children in school. The total cost of primary education proved to be approximately £10 (₦20) a head a year. The government grant was fixed at £6 (now ₦12 a head), leaving the remainder to be found from local resources, that is from fees or taxes or a combination of both. This has proved a strong incentive for local authorities to be economical in their expenditure and to encourage children of school age to enter their local school since government grants are fixed and the local contribution is residual.

A significant increase in primary school enrolment was achieved.

Primary School Enrolment

	Male	*Female*	*Total*
1959	184,522	66,390	150,912
1960	206,443	76,405	282,849
1961	230,500	85,764	316,264
1962	262,083	97,851	359,934
1963	295,644	115,062	410,706
1964	323,399	128,920	452,319
1965	381,900	152,300	534,200

In less than eight years, the increase was well over 100 per cent. In addition to these considerable increases in roll, more pupils completed their courses as wastage declined. The main reason for this was that the division between junior and senior primary schools had been removed.[11]

NOTES

1 Sir Eric Ashby, *Investment in Education, Report of the Commission on Post-School Certificate and Higher Education in Nigeria* (Lagos, Nigeria: Government Printer 1960), p. 2.

2 Ibid., pp. 10-47.

3 Government of Northern Nigeria, *White Paper on Education Development in Northern Nigeria* (Kaduna: The Government Printer, 1961), pp. 1-10.

4 H. Oldman, *The Administration of Primary Education* (Kaduna: Government Printer, 1961), pp. 5-6.

5 Ibid., pp. 28-30.

6 Government Printer, *Education Law of Northern Nigeria, 1964* (Kaduna: Government Printer, 1964).

7 Ibid.

8 Ministry of Education, *Education in the Six Northern States of Nigeria, 1962-73* (Kaduna: Baraka Press Ltd., November, 1967), pp. 15-48.

9 Ibid.

10 Ibid.

11 Ibid.

SUMMARY OF PART ONE

Education Ordinance 1916

The total number of children in school in the northern provinces in 1912 was only 954. In the South there were 35,716 children in school in the same year. By 1926, the children in the northern schools increased to 5,210 as compared with 138,248 in the South. The increase of over 400 per cent for the northern provinces was very high. However, the gap between the North and South was still very wide: 5,210 to 138,248.

Northern Nigerians were not trained for clerical jobs and this led to the influx of qualified people from the South, Gold Coast (Ghana) and Sierra Leone who came to take on the jobs.

Vischer's educational experiment which the 1916 Ordinance sought to protect did not work entirely in the interests of the people.

The 1916 Ordinance encouraged educational expansion in the South and slowed down comparatively the educational development in the North.

Education Ordinance 1926

The great slump in international trade greatly limited the success of the aims the ordinance set out to achieve: *(1)* co-operation with voluntary agencies by means of increased subsidies to schools and training institutions, and *(2)* an attempt to improve the quality and status of teachers.

Its positive effect was greatly felt in the pagan areas of the North. For in 1926, there were a little over 5,000 primary school enrollees and by 1947 the enrolment had climbed to approximately 71,000.

The teachers in the mission schools benefitted most since the greater part of the grants-in-aid went to pay the salaries of qualified instructors.

The government stressed quality and the need for better

qualified teachers with the result that it raised the standards for teacher qualification.

Education Ordinance 1948

The Ten-Year Development Plan for Nigeria was revised and its items regionalized.

Native authorities could not open projected schools due to shortage of teachers. A large number of teachers were engaged in political activities, which the ordinance did not forbid, with the result that their services were lost for considerable periods each year.

Junior secondary schools replaced middle schools in the North.

The first appeal was one against the witholding of consent to open a Sudan Interior Mission School at Matazu in Katsina Province: it was successful. The principle involved the right of a Christian community to establish its own school in a Muslim area.

The compulsory attendance law could be invoked by native authorities.

The new salary scale severely affected the unassisted mission schools where teachers were paid lower salaries than their counterparts in assisted schools.

There were three salary scales operating in the region—government, native authority and voluntary agency. This gave rise to dissatisfaction.

Ordinances were at last printed and made available for issue to the school managers.

There was great increase in school enrolment. In 1949 only one child in twenty-six was in school, four years later, one in every seventeen was receiving some form of primary education. There were, therefore, half as many more children in school than there were five years before.

The voluntary agencies still appeared to be shouldering the greater responsibility for education.

Education Ordinance 1956

The Ministry of Education was reorganized in connection with a process known as 'Integration'. As a result the Department of Education which existed in the North since 1910, ceased to exist as such and was merged with the Ministry of Education.

The offices of the Director and Deputy Director also ceased to exist and the holders of these two offices were appointed respectively as Adviser and Chief Inspector of Education, the latter assuming charge of the newly formed Inspectorate Division of the ministry. The executive control of the ministry passed to the Permanent Secretary who was assisted by a deputy. The holders of these offices were Administrative Officers.

The difference between the educational development of the riverain provinces and that of the 'Far Northern' provinces began to be more noticed and emphasized.

A new seven-year primary school syllabus was introduced. This replaced the former four-year primary followed by the three-year middle school syllabus previously used in the region and the 'southern' eight-year syllabus which was used by some of the voluntary agencies.

With the increase in the number of schools, it became noticeable that no fees were paid in government schools. Nominal fees were paid in native authority schools and fees were collected in all voluntary agency schools.

Education Ordinance 1962

The powers of the Minister of Education were clearly stated in the Ordinance in the light of the powers conferred by the constitution.

There were changes in the Ministry and in the provinces. The Chief Education Officer (General) became Senior Inspector of Primary Schools and a post of Deputy Senior Inspector of Primary Schools was created.

In the provinces, the posts of Area Inspectors were abolished together with the posts of Provincial Education Officers. The duties of Provincial Education Officers were divided into two: Inspection and Administration. The posts of Provincial Inspectors of Education and Provincial Education Secretaries were created—the former to carry out the inspection and to deal with professional matters and the latter to deal with administration of schools.

Forty-six local education authorities were set up. The remaining eight local education authorities were created in 1968, so that all the primary schools within the six northern states were then administered by local education authorities.

The system of grant-aiding primary education was changed. It was henceforth to be based on Oldman's recommendations.

There was a significant increase in primary school enrolment. In less than eight years the increase was well over 100 per cent. In addition to the increase in roll, more pupils completed their courses as wastage declined. The division between junior and senior primary schools was removed.

PART TWO

5

THE IMPLICATIONS FOR NORTHERN NIGERIA

IT IS important to examine in detail the following points which have significant implications for education in Northern Nigeria: *(1)* voluntary agencies, *(2)* control of education, *(3)* the teacher and the teaching profession, *(4)* curriculum, and *(5)* administration and financing of education in Northern Nigeria.

VOLUNTARY AGENCIES

The role played by the missions, more often referred to as the voluntary agencies, in the educational development of Northern Nigeria has achieved very positive results as the preceding chapters have revealed. All the same, their role has been the subject of different reactions from different quarters. Dr. A.D. Galloway, formerly Professor of Religious Studies at the University College, Ibadan, had the following to say:

> In spite of their pietistic theology, the early Missionaries came from a culture which kept only one eye fixed on heaven, while the other was focused quite firmly on the earth. Though the comforts of this world were regarded as possible distractions from an ultimate heavenly testing, yet at the same time they were regarded as indications of the goodness and providence of God. . . . Therefore, in the first human relations between Britain and Nigeria, the sharp distinction between Mission and Trade was not strictly observed.[1]

Some people looked upon missionary activities as a concomitant of British Imperialism. Chief Dennis Osadebey, formerly Premier of the Mid-Western State of Nigeria described the situation in the following words:

> The Missionary has made the African soil fertile for the growth of imperialism . . . (but) he has equally helped to lay the foundations for the present spirit of nationalism . . . when African historians come to write their own account of the adventure of Africa with Imperialism, they will write of the Missionaries as the greatest friends the African had.[2]

Mr. P.O. Okeke, Principal of Our Lady's High School, Onitsha, had the following to say about the curricular offerings of the early missionary education in Nigeria:

> The earliest schools in Nigeria were modelled along the lines of these charity schools. The curriculum was overweighted with religious knowledge–recitation of the catechism, reading passages from the Bible and singing hymns. When the songs were not religious they had to be in praise of Britain or of British scenery or of an episode in British history–'Rule Britannia', 'D' ye ken John Peel', 'Bonnie Charlie', 'Ye Banks an' Braes', etc. Since the emphasis was on softening the minds of the 'wild' children, religious instruction was reinforced by moral lessons on virtue, charity, humility, courage and truthfulness. Some reading, writing and arithmetic were added to the school curriculum.[3]

On the other hand, Professor L.J. Lewis of the Institute of Education, London University, commented on the situation as follows:

> In attempting to pass judgement on the work of this initial period of unco-ordinated activity, it is important to refrain from judging wisely after the event. It must be recognized that, despite the apparent deficiencies, such education as was provided not only produced an excellent cadre of local assistants for state and church, but also a number of outstanding individuals. In addition, among the educated population there was created a quality of public opinion, which on occasion exercised considerable influence to the advantage of those in authority. It is, in fact, in terms of the lives and characters of individuals rather than in terms of policy and organization that the educational effort of this period is to be judged.[4]

Be that as it may, the question still to be answered is how did the voluntary agencies come to play such a big part in Northern Nigerian education, especially in view of Lugard's assurances to the Muslim emirates and the early attempts of the Colonial Office in London and Hanns Vischer to stop their expansion. R.J. Mason supplied the answer when he said:

> It is not surprising that the British brought their educational philosophy and their pattern of organization to Africa, especially as the coming of the British to Africa coincided with a period of great religious activity in England which resulted in the formation of a number of missionary societies. The relationship between the State or Government, and the Voluntary Agencies in Africa has followed very much the pattern of that in England, and development in England has conditioned development in Africa.[5]

Sir Eric Ashby, in his comments on overseas British policy on higher education had the following to say:

> Underlying British Enterprise in providing higher education for her people Overseas was one massive assumption that the pattern of University appropriate for Manchester, Exeter and Hull was *ipso facto* appropriate for Ibadan, Kampala and Singapore. If we were going to export Universities to our Overseas dependencies, they would of course be British Universities, just as the cars we export there are British cars. As with cars, so with Universities. We willingly made minor modifications to suit the climate, but we did not regard it as our business to enquire whether French or American models might be more suitable.[6]

It would appear therefore that the attempts of Hanns Vischer and the British Colonial Office to restrict through the education ordinances the missionary activities in the field of education in the northern provinces had to fail in the long run. The reason being that the British Colonial Officers ended up doing precisely what they best knew how to do at home, working and co-operating with the voluntary agencies. Hence Section 2 of the Education Ordinance of 1916 defines 'School' as 'an institution in which more than ten pupils are systematically taught, and in which any person is engaged to impart education'; and for 'Proprietor' we have: 'Proprietor in relation to a school means any person, society or corporation by whom or which a non-Government school is established or conducted'. In Section 3, the ordinance maintains that 'The Governor may from time to time establish Government schools in Nigeria'. This situation might have led to *(1)* the evolution of 'dual control' in the operation of the schools in Northern Nigeria as was the case in Britain, *(2)* the uneven educational development between the riverain areas of Northern Nigeria, and the 'Far North' Muslim areas of Northern Nigeria, and *(3)* the division of teachers and the teaching profession into different categories: civil service, voluntary agency teachers and native authority teachers.

CONTROL OF EDUCATION

This is a very topical subject in Nigeria today. The state governments of the federation have proposed various policies, some bordering on complete take-over of schools. The take-overs have not been in the same form with all the governments and the public reaction to the whole exercise has not been easy to identify. The question that should first be asked is, what is the true position about the control of schools in Nigeria up till now?

The history of education in Nigeria reveals the following trends of development:

(a) Missionaries were the first to establish schools on their own initiative in the early nineteenth century. This was dictated by the exigencies of their undertaking. Converts had to be able to read the scriptures.

(b) The government at first encouraged the missionaries and later enacted education ordinances to control, regulate and partly finance education under the management of voluntary agencies.

(c) In the South, the pattern was that of expansion in which the missions were encouraged to spread into the interior while the pattern in the North was that of restricted expansion.

(d) Both in the southern and northern provinces, the government was faced with the problem of education of the Muslim children. This led to the government providing its own schools directly in Lagos and in the northern provinces.

From this brief survey, it can be seen that the voluntary agencies (missionaries in fact) had control of their schools only at the initial stages when they were neither encumbered by Education Laws nor by grants-in-aid regulations. The most obvious deduction therefore is that from the promulgation of the 1916 Education Ordinance up till now, the control of education has been primarily in the hands of government, and the voluntary agencies were in fact agents helping in the administration and management of schools. This is an important distinction that must be clearly understood in our consideration of this important topic. No individual or organization can start a school in Nigeria without conforming to set regulations. Any school in Nigeria is open to government inspection with or without prior notice. The government determines the kind and number of teachers in schools and has the right to order the closure of any school. These facts should leave no room for doubt about the seat of power and control of schools.

The important aspect of schools in Nigeria that should be remembered is that the day-to-day administration of schools has been shared up till now by both the governments and voluntary agencies who acted as proprietors of schools. Such schools have tended to adopt some set patterns or tone depending upon who the proprietor was. We are therefore confronted with as many different religions and as many different rates of school fees as there are Proprietors. All these are presumably carried out on behalf of the governments that provide the funds wholly or in part.

This is not a trend of development peculiar to Nigeria. The educational development in Britain and the United States of America are not too dissimilar to ours at the initial stages. They all started under missionary zeal and were run by voluntary agencies.

THE TEACHER AND THE TEACHING PROFESSION

As the review of literature on the ordinances in Chapter Two has shown, there were three categories of school management in Northern Nigeria: *(1)* schools under the local education authorities, mainly primary schools, *(2)* secondary schools and teachers colleges run by voluntary agencies, and *(3)* secondary schools, teacher-training and technical colleges operated directly by the government. This tripartite school management situation has led to an unjustified classification of teachers which has discriminated against certain teachers who have identical qualifications but different salaries and professional names.[7]

Teachers in government institutions are civil servants and therefore have their salaries and promotion geared to the different sectors of the civil service. It is not unusual therefore, for a teacher entering the civil service, say as a Grade I teacher, to rise by promotion to the administrative position of the Chief Inspector of Education or Permanent Secretary without obtaining additional academic qualifications.[8] This type of situation did not apply to the voluntary agency teachers for whom there were no promotion ladders and whose salaries were strictly based on academic qualifications stipulated by the government. For the purposes of illustration, a Grade I teacher working for a voluntary agency could never be expected to earn more than ₦1710 per annum unless he acquired higher qualifications. His counterpart with identical qualifications who joined the civil service and remained in the classroom as a teacher could rise to the status of Senior Education Officer on a salary of ₦2736, (1973 figures). Over and above this, the teacher-civil servant could get promoted to such administrative positions as Provincial Inspector of Education and Chief Inspector; posts which were not open to the teacher working for the voluntary agency. The salary of a Chief Inspector of Education is ₦4938, approximately three times the salary of the Grade I voluntary agency teacher.

The teacher under the local authority was not as well-off as the teacher working for the government but he was better-off than the teacher in a voluntary agency school. The local authority teacher could transfer his services to the civil service with his seniority intact. This did not apply to the voluntary agency teacher.

Certain remarks of Governor Sir Arthur Richards are not only pertinent but revealing. He said with regard to teachers working in voluntary agency schools whose salaries were grant-aided by the government:

> There are, indeed, some unhealthy features in the present administration of the Grant. . . . Another substantial slice goes to the payment or part payment of teachers' salaries and cost of living allowance. Now although these payments are made to the Agencies and not directly to the teachers it was almost inevitable that the latter should come to regard themselves as quasi-civil servants. They have in fact done so and lay increasing emphasis on their rights and claims on Government. This is not a happy state of affairs for although Government may accept a moral obligation to help these teachers it is not proper that it should be pressed to treat as its servants those over whom it has so little control.[9]

With regard to the working conditions of voluntary agency teachers, Governor Richards went on to say:

> Government has lately extended its educational responsibilities by publishing a scheme for the superannuation of non-Government teachers. Broadly speaking this scheme is in line with that adopted for Government servants. It provides, subject to certain qualifications and safeguards, that a certificated teacher who retires on a salary of £50 (₦100) or more shall become eligible for an annual allowance and that one who retires on a lesser salary shall be eligible for a gratuity based on the length of his service.[10]

However, of government teachers, he had the following to say:

> Government teachers, for their part, have shown an increasing disposition to regard themselves as a separate caste and do not coalesce readily with other members of

> their profession. . . . It would make for greater harmony in the teaching profession if the scales of Government and non-Government teachers approximated more closely.

All that can be deduced from the Governor's remarks is that he did not advocate equal pay and conditions of service for all the teachers. For on conditions of service for voluntary agency teachers, he maintained that 'It is not proper that it (the government) should be pressed to treat as its servants those over whom it has so little control', and on superannuation schemes for the same teachers, he went further to say, 'Broadly speaking this scheme is in line with that adopted for Government servants'. In other words, the schemes were not identical. Where the Governor wanted harmony among the government teachers and the voluntary agency teachers, he suggested that 'It would make for greater harmony . . . if the scales of Government and non-Government teachers approximated more closely'. He was still not advocating equality of pay.

A situation such as this could never allow for the flexibility needed to give teachers adequate remuneration commensurate with their output. For they were either tied down to civil service salary scales or to discriminatory government salary regulations. This might have accounted for the lack of a truly virile representative teachers' professional organization in Nigeria. It could also account for the lack of interest in teaching as a profession in Nigeria. A change in the management of Nigerian schools is required to bring about equitable conditions of service for all teachers.

In Section 2 of the 1916 Education Ordinance, there is the definition: 'Staff—In relation to a school means all persons engaged in teaching in the school'. A closer examination of the subsequent education ordinances will reveal that teachers were categorized to include all sorts. For example, there were vernacular teachers, probationary teachers, untrained teachers, trained uncertificated teachers, handicraft teachers, technical teachers, graduate teachers with no teaching qualifications, Grade IV, III, II and I teachers, and N.C.E. teachers *ad infinitum*.

These teachers range from primary school leavers, to those who went through secondary schools, teacher training colleges, technical colleges, and even right through the university. In each case there is room for pass/fail candidates to enter teaching. This situation tends to confirm the statement attributed to Bernard Shaw: 'If you can, do; if you can't, teach'.

In the other professions such as medicine or engineering, failures are not allowed to practice. It is becoming increasingly clear that to surrender children to 'teachers' who have no knowledge of child psychology and no understanding of the sociological background of the child and other factors that could motivate or impede learning is tantamount to a person subjecting himself to surgical operation by a butcher just because he happens to be in possession of a knife.

The result has been the same in each case—death. Many children have literally been condemned as nincompoops just because their teachers were not sufficiently informed to reach out to them and draw out the best that was in them.

If teachers therefore wish to be respected by the public, they must project a respectable image and one way of doing this is to rid the teaching profession of failures.

THE CURRICULUM

After the First World War, the American Baptist Mission decided that, in planning for postwar development, a thorough study of the existing situation in Africa was essential as the first step. A commission of inquiry, headed by Dr. Jesse Jones and including an African member, Dr. James Aggrey of the Gold Coast (Ghana) and Columbia University, left for Africa in 1920. The commission was financed by the Phelps-Stokes fund, a trust established to further the education of Negroes in Africa and the United States.[12]

The commission found educated Africans already occupying 'positions of importance' in every colony visited and it was impressed by the potentialities shown. But the educational policies of governments and missions alike seemed inadequate and 'largely unreal so far as the vital needs of Africans are concerned'. It criticized the view that 'a curriculum well suited to the needs of a group on a given scale of civilization in one country is necessarily the best for other groups on a different level of advancement in another country'. The commission made detailed suggestions as to how education could be adapted to the needs of African society, 'so as to promote its development without causing its disruption'.[13]

Following the recommendations of the Phelps-Stokes Commission the Advisory Committee on Native Education in Tropical Africa was set up in 1923 'to advise the Secretary of State on any matters . . . which he may from time to time refer to it, and to assist him in advancing the progress of education in the Colonies and Protectorate'. In 1925, it brought out its memorandum which became a landmark in the history of education in the colonies. The committee outlined the following broad principles:

(1) Government welcomes and will encourage all voluntary educational efforts which conform to the general policy.

(2) Education should be adapted to the mentality, aptitudes, occupations and traditions of the various peoples, care must be taken to avoid creating a hiatus between the educated class and the rest of the community.

(3) A thorough system of supervision and inspection is indispensable for the vitality and efficiency of the system.

(4) So far as local conditions permit, women's and girls' education must be attempted wherever possible, care must be taken however, to see that such an education does not have an unsettling effect upon the people of the country.[14]

On very close examination of all the suggestions put forward by both the Phelps-Stokes Commission and the Advisory Committee on Native Education in Tropical Areas (incidentally, Hanns Vischer was the secretary of the committee), one is bound to conclude that there was close resemblance between these suggestions and the principles underlying the education ordinances which Lugard and the subsequent

Governors introduced to Nigeria. Indeed, these suggestions could be identified with what Hanns Vischer set out to do in Northern Nigeria where according to him:

> The system of education should endeavour to educate without, if possible, in any way damaging their racial feeling or separating them from their parents or their surroundings. . . . The technical instruction is intended to produce efficient artisans not dependent on European machinery.[15]

The question to raise at this juncture is how did practice relate to theory? It was true that Vischer insisted not only on a breakaway from the tyranny of foreign school examinations and diplomas but also tried to relate his curriculum to the Northern Nigerian environment.

However, Vischer's method of adaptation precluded relevancy. He insisted on local crafts to the exclusion of modern machinery at the time modern means of transportation—railways, motor cars—and mercantile houses were making their impact on Northern Nigeria. He did not prepare Northern Nigerians for overseas examinations and diplomas while the government departments with which Vischer himself was associated would not employ Nigerians unless they possessed those very overseas diplomas.[16] Okuorah Okeke recently commented on the situation as follows:

> There is a second major problem, that of the WAEC School Certificate which every secondary school child strives to acquire as a passport to government employment. As long as the incentive is there—a civil service job—there is no way to break the vicious circle, however much we desire to do so. No policy paper has yet been adopted which would divorce the Secondary School Certificate from civil service employment.[17]

By denying the Northern Nigerians this type of education and allowing Southerners with those same certificates to come to the North for employment, while they lived in segregated areas, was not only unfair to the Northerners who were made to look educationally inferior, but it also undermined the economy of the North and laid the foundation of mistrust, jealousy and unhealthy rivalry among the Northerners and Southerners which ultimately led to the recent civil war.[18]

It is because of this apparent contradiction in government's policy and practice that one is bound to disagree with D.H. Williams when he said:

> And it was the people themselves who misguidedly perhaps, created a demand for a more academic and a less practical system in which their children should be educated.[19]

The Phelps-Stokes Commission Report of 1922 made the following remarks on adaptation:

> Past experience has convinced some of the educated Natives that departure from the white man's methods have too frequently meant an inferior provision for the black people. They are naturally suspicious of adoptions as the entering wedge for educational segregation. Any movement to provide an inferior system of education for the black man is of course to be condemned. Study of recent movements in education should quickly convince the Africans and their friends that adaptation provides for all phases of education, from the elementary school to the specialized professions, that are required for the full development of the African people.[20]

It is in the light of the foregoing that the deliberations of the National Curriculum Conference which met in Lagos on 8-12 September 1969 should be regarded as very important in the review of any future education ordinance. It was a conference which was attended by a cross-section of the people of Nigeria. For the first time, it was possible for Nigerians to deliberate, by themselves, on the aims and goals of education suited for their children. The kind of philosophy that should guide the country's education was clearly articulated, and the scope of the conference can be seen from the chapter headings of the book of the conference proceedings:[21]

Chapter I The Purpose of Primary Education
II The Purpose of Secondary Education
III The Purpose of University Education
IV Teachers' Education
V Education of Women
VI Education for Living
VII The Role of Science and Technology in National Development.
VIII A Summary of Issues and Recommendations.

The recommendations made at the conference have formed the guide for the major review of curriculum activities that is being carried out at the Nigerian Educational Research Council and the various curriculum development centres in Nigerian Universities.

The following are some significant recommendations on curriculum that came out of the National Curriculum Conference:

Primary Education

(1) A six-year primary education course is required. Children normally enter at the age of six and leave at twelve;

(2) State control and management of primary education becomes imperative now, i.e. the voluntary agencies should transfer the schools to the government. Private schools may still open if they satisfy minimum regulations;

(3) In the event of State control of primary schools, these schools should become Community Schools, thus becoming the intellectual, aesthetic and social centres of the community;

(4) The Nigerian primary school child should be grounded in his/her mother tongue apart from learning English and or any other language as a second or third language;

(5) The existing curriculum should de-emphasize examination-centredness to permit the schools to function properly. . .

Secondary Education

(1) We need a secondary education that will combine academic training with practical and vocational orientation.

(2) Whether multi-lateral or comprehensive, the school must be large enough to offer a diversified curriculum rich in quantity and quality to satisfy the learning ambitions of each child and the societal needs.

(3) All pupils should be exposed to a core curriculum of basic learning and specialized curricula offerings.

(4) Emphasis should be given to character training and practical training for all according to aptitude and ability, particularly in the areas of agriculture, home economics, vocational training and aesthetic appreciation.

(5) The secondary school, like the primary school, should be a community school.

These points only go to emphasize that the Nigerians have discovered how inappropriate and irrelevant the existing curriculum is at all levels, but they also suggest some practical ways of improving the situation. These philosophies will have to be incorporated in our educational policies and be implemented through reformed education laws.

Now that our objectives have been put into focus, it requires very realistic planning, effective teacher training and intensive in-service training of teachers to achieve these goals. The new education ordinance must take into account all these aspects as well. Indeed the National Curriculum Conference of 1969 made specific recommendations on the subject of teachers.

Teacher Education

(i) Purposes of Teacher Education:

(1) To produce a highly motivated, conscientious and successful classroom teacher for all levels of our education system;

(2) To encourage further the spirit of inquiry, creativity, nationalism and belongingness;

(3) To help the prospective teacher to fit into the social life of his home, his immediate and non-immediate communities;

(4) To provide him with an intellectual and professional background adequate for his assignment and adaptable to any changing situation in the life of his country;

(5) In sum, to produce knowledgeable, progressive and effective teachers who can inspire children to learn.

(ii) Recommendations:

(1) Nigeria requires well-trained and well-groomed teachers in her classrooms, therefore we must intensify the preparation of teacher training colleges; and the preparation of the prospective teachers themselves.

(2) The student teacher should have a minimum educational background of School Certificate or its equivalent before entry to a teacher training college. In the interim, candidates with less academic qualifications can be encouraged to train as teachers for a longer period of about five or six years to get academic and professional training.

(3) A three or four year period of training at the University level is required to earn a degree as a qualified graduate teacher.

(4) The B.A./B.Sc.(Education) or B.Ed. degree structure was preferred. Candidates with a liberal arts degree in arts or science can be encouraged to take a Diploma Course to qualify as a graduate teacher.

(5) The N.C.E. Syllabus should be upgraded to ensure the original status conceived for it, that is, as a level much above the H.S.C. but a little below the first degree level.

(6) The teacher education programme should consist of a satisfactory blending between:

- *(a)* the general education of the teacher
- *(b)* his academic preparations, and
- *(c)* his professional training.

(7) That the possibility of a probation system of prospective teachers should be considered on its own merit for the production of competent teachers.

(8) A longer student-teaching practice period must be used to strengthen the professional preparation of the teacher.

(9) There is need to reduce the categories of qualified and unqualified teachers in Nigeria. Three such categories are proposed:

- *(a)* qualified teachers: graduates with a teaching qualification not below N.C.E. or Dip. Ed. or a degree in education, or non-graduates but well qualified N.C.E. teachers.
- *(b)* Intermediate Cadet Teachers: Grade II and I certificated teachers.
- *(c)* Unqualified teachers: all others.

(10) Teaching as a profession must not be designed as a dead-end for prospective teachers. They should be encouraged with promotional prospects within the levels of their training in order to reduce the teacher turnover rate. The Conference would like to see well-qualified teachers train in the area of:

- *(a)* pre-primary or primary education;
- *(b)* secondary education, with specialization in one or two subject areas;
- *(c)* special teachers for specific children, e.g. the deaf and dumb, the blind, etc.

(11) Teachers' Unions must strive to raise their own status through professionalization of teaching and more positive work in the area of educational research.

(12) In-service training and re-training of teachers must be done on a continuous basis with a mind to:

- *(a)* improving teacher effectiveness in the classroom
- *(b)* encouraging him through further incentives for additional experience gained.

(13) There is need for a continuous assessment of the teacher trainee in all aspects of his work throughout the course rather than a dependence on the current practice of a final examination at the very end of the teachers' course.

(14) Training Programmes must aim at the concept of relevance, balance and functionalism to make them worthwhile. They must be geared to the needs of the teacher and the level of education for which he is being prepared.

(15) More effective supervision is called for. Perhaps the best

supervision is self evaluation and a systematic evaluation from the headmaster on the spot. Inspectors of education should make more frequent visits to help teachers. In this regard, there is need for more and better qualified inspectorate staff to make it possible for more frequent visits to classrooms to help individual teachers that need such professional assistance.

(16) Teachers' Colleges must be consolidated to make them all-purpose institutions for the realization of our teacher training objectives.

(17) Prospects of further training should be built into the teacher education structure; this implies a built-in remuneration system as a sort of professional incentive to the teacher.

(18) Certification of teachers should be a national function through a Joint Matriculation Board of the Universities or a similar apparatus within the Federal Ministry of Education.

(19) The Headmastership should become a professional qualification earned through a period of academic and professional training to prepare the incumbent for his new roles as guide and supervisor in an atmosphere for creating effective teaching and learning situations and opportunities in our schools.

(20) There ought to be more consultations with teacher organizations and associations on education policy determination.

CURRICULUM CHANGE

The aims, objectives and recommendations of the National Curriculum Conference all go to show the good intentions of Nigerians. There has been full realization of the need to change the school curriculum to reflect more clearly national aspirations and needs, and to remove completely unacceptable carry-overs of colonial education policies and systems. Good intentions alone will not do. There must be follow-up, and constructive planning supported by adequate finance, men and materials.

The National Conference has been followed up by a Workshop on the Primary Curriculum in April 1971, and followed by another Workshop on Primary Teacher Training in April 1972. Development of experimental materials has been carried out at various places to various extents. A large scheme for the development of primary curriculum materials is centred at the Institute of Education, Ahmadu Bello University. This was made possible by a UNESCO/UNICEF Grant of ₦5 million and it is supposed to cover the primary schools in the six Northern States of Nigeria. The Science Teachers' Association for Nigeria with the support of the Ford Foundation assisted the Comparative Education Study and Adaptation Centre of the University of Lagos in developing a properly tested curriculum for secondary science. These are two of the many curricula activities going on at the moment. As can be appreciated from these two examples, if Nigeria is to translate her plans into action she must review the administrative and financial provisions made to implement them.

FINANCING OF EDUCATION

The administration and financing of education in Northern Nigeria can be divided into: *(1)* elementary schools financed by the government and the local people, based on Oldman's recommendations, *(2)* secondary schools and teachers' colleges financed by government grants; or private contributions and fees for those run by the voluntary agencies, and *(3)* government secondary schools and technical colleges heavily subsidized by government, though minimal fees paid on a sliding scale based on roughly assessed earning capacities of parents or guardians are sometimes paid. No fees are charged in teachers' colleges run by the government. Instead students are paid pocket money and other allowances.[22]

The development of the administration of primary education from the 'dual control' system to the eventual take-over by the local education authorities has been reviewed in Chapter 2. However, the financing of primary education as recommended by Oldman and adopted by the Northern Regional Government will need to be carefully assessed. The total cost of primary education was calculated to be approximately ₦20 a head a year. The government grant was arbitrarily fixed at ₦10 (now ₦12) a head leaving the remainder to be found from local sources, that is, from fees or taxes or a combination of both.[23]

Although this might be regarded as a simpler computation than the Phillipson formula which was formerly applied in grant-aiding schools according to Education Ordinance 1948, it has already been realized in many parts of Northern Nigeria that the cost of ₦20 per head was very much an under estimate. Apart from this, the newly formed local education authorities do not all have the same financial commitments. In some areas, this unhealthy situation has led to the exodus of experienced teachers whose salaries could not be paid by their local education authorities. Expansion has been halted in many other areas for the same reason.

To remedy such deficiencies, not only is it imperative that the total cost of primary education be accurately re-assessed, but it is also important that the policy of a block grant of ₦12 per head should be reviewed so that a policy of grant commensurate with the wealth of the different local education authorities can be applied. The American system of a equalization plan could be applied with some modifications. According to Morphet and Johns:

> To carry into effect the principle of equalization of schools' support, as commonly understood, it would be necessary *(1)* To establish schools or make other arrangements sufficient to furnish the children in every locality within the state with equal educational opportunities up to some prescribed minimum. *(2)* To raise the funds necessary for this purpose by local or state taxation adjusted in such manner as to bear upon the people in all localities at the same rate in relation to their taxing ability, and *(3)* To provide adequately for the supervision and control of all the schools by a state department of education. The simplest method of financing schools to achieve the aim of the principle would be through uniform state-wide taxes on ability to pay.[24]

Lewis and Loveridge maintain that except in very sophisticated societies, equalization is difficult for it requires the possession of very precise knowledge regarding the wealth that can be tapped in every part of the society in addition to a precise idea of what is reasonable expenditure upon the desirable education of a child.[25] To agree readily with this opinion is to dismiss easily the application of this principle to other places with similar problems. The use of the phrase 'very sophisticated societies' is, of course, very loose and lacks any scientific objectivity. In Northern Nigeria, a study as to what constitutes the cost of a minimum desirable programme of education to be offered to every child was undertaken following Oldman's report. The details of this have been discussed earlier on. Experience has shown that the ₦20 estimated was adequate in some parts of Northern Nigeria and not in others. The next step is to review the situation in the light of new developments. The problem of assessment of the wealth that can be tapped is not insurmountable in the Northern Nigerian situation. The local authorities keep a register of all landed properties in townships and collect annual rents on them based on assessed valuation of the properties. Taxes are based on income wherever possible, and in villages rates are applied. With all these potentials at the disposal of the local authorities, it should be possible to organize further assessments on an almost accurate basis. The central government can come to the aid of any local authority that runs into difficulty by supplying qualified assessors. It might be worthwhile for the government to investigate the possibility of introducing the system of an 'Equalization Plan'.

The gradual withdrawal of government from the management of schools and the eventual take over of all schools by representative local education authorities should enable the financing of educational programmes to be properly co-ordinated and reasonably decentralized and localized.

The same should apply to secondary schools and post-primary institutions as they become part of the local education authority system.

To apply an equalization plan to full advantage, it will be necessary for both state and federal governments to evolve a system so that the situation will not arise where a state government or a local authority will have to spend a greater share of its revenue on education at the expense of other social services. An equalization plan would enable governments to make arrangements to furnish children in every locality within the state with equal educational opportunities up to a prescribed minimum standard. The governments could agree on what percentage of total revenue could be spent on different aspects of social services. If any local authority was found spending above the agreed percentage in order to provide education up to the prescribed minimum, that local authority could receive reimbursement for whatever it spent over and above the fixed percentage. The same system could operate between the state and federal governments. Where any state spent a greater percentage of its revenue on education over and above a fixed level the federal government could fully reimburse the state for the over-expenditure incurred.

For example, a state government might fix the prescribed minimum education in its area as education up to primary 4 for every child of the state. To achieve this minimum, the government would agree that each local authority was expected to spend 20 per cent of its social estimates for the year on education in order to provide this minimum standard. Wherever any local authority was forced by its peculiar circumstances to spend 35 per cent of its revenue to achieve this minimum, it should be the responsibility of the state government to reimburse the local authority for the excess 15 per cent. This is a crude illustration of the equalization plan in practice.

One obvious advantage of an equalization plan is that both state and federal governments are in a position to help furnish children in every locality within the federation with equal educational opportunities up to some prescribed minimum standard without making it impossible for the local authority or the state government to carry out adequately their responsibilities for providing other social amenities as well.

NOTES

1 A. D. Galloway, 'Missionary Impact on Nigeria', *Nigeria, A Special*

Independence Issue of Nigeria Magazine October 1960 (Lagos: Federal Ministry of Information, Printing Division, 1960) p. 59.

2 Ibid.

3 Okechukwu Ikejiani, *Education in Nigeria* (New York: Frederick A. Praeger, 1965), p. 43.

4 L. J. Lewis, *Educational Policy and Practice in British Tropical Areas* (London: Thomas Nelson and Sons Ltd., 1954), p. 13.

5 R. J. Mason, *British Education in Africa* (London; Oxford University Press, 1959), p. 21.

6 Sir Eric Ashby, *Universities: British, Indian, African* (Cambridge, Massachusetts: Harvard University Press, 1966), p. 224.

7 Government Printer, *'Education Law of Northern Nigeria 1964'* (Kaduna: Government Printer), pp. 32-35.

8 Government Printer, *Staff List, 1962* (Kaduna: Government Printer).

9 Ibid., p. 54.

10 Ibid.

11 Ibid.

12 'Education in Africa', (New York: Phelps-Stokes Fund, 1922), p. xxiii.

13 Ibid., p. 38.

14 British Information Services, *Education in the U.K. Dependencies* (London: Cox and Sharland Ltd., May, 1959), pp. 9-11.

15 Williams, op. cit., pp. 19-20.

16 Graham, op. cit., pp. 148-152.

17 Ikejiani, op. cit., p. 8.

18 Waugh and Cronje, loc. cit.

19 Williams, op. cit., pp. 19-20.

20 David G. Scalon, *Traditions of African Education* (Columbia University, N.Y.: Bureau of Publications, Teachers College, 1964), p. 56.

21 Adeniyi Adaralegbe, *A Philosophy for Nigerian Education* (Heinemann Educational Books (Nigeria) Ltd. Ibadan, 1972).

22 Annual Report, 1954-55, op. cit., p. 8.

23 Education in the Six Northern States, 1962-73, op. cit., p. 47.

24 Edgar L. Morphet and Roe L. Johns, *Financing the Public Schools* (Englewood Cliffs, N.J.: Prentice-Hall, Inc., 1960), pp. 263-264.

25 Lewis and Loveridge, op. cit., pp. 85-86.

6

THE WAY AHEAD

IT HAS been established that the problems now confronting Northern Nigeria (the six Northern States of Nigeria) require a thorough review of the education ordinances to bring them in line with the educational philosophy and objectives of the people. For example, the National Curriculum Conference of September, 1969, came out clearly on the side of State control and management of schools. It went further to maintain that such schools must become community schools, centres of intellectual, aesthetic and social activities of the community. It was agreed that primary schools should place less emphasis on examinations. The new education ordinance must take notice of all these recommendations, especially as they relate to teacher-qualification, and composition of Education Boards and School Committees.

The local education authorities can be democratized and given overall control of educational programmes in their areas of jurisdiction. The temptation following the recommendations of the National Curriculum Conference on control of schools is for the State governments to bring all schools under direct management of governments. This would not only be totalitarian but would surely lead to a situation where the governments will constitute themselves into proprietors and inspectors at the same time. Government control should not necessarily mean direct government management of schools. The local education authorities could be strengthened and improved upon to enable them to perform their functions more efficiently and so take on added responsibilities.

The education ordinances must take into account the constitutional safeguards for the religious rights of Nigerian citizens. With the governments' take-over of schools, the implications of this constitutional right must not be lost sight of. The problem is how is a government to make provision for the wide variety of religious beliefs? Some countries such as the U.S.S.R. and the U.S.A. have decided to drop religious dogmas from school curricula. The U.S.A. based its decision on the American constitution. The Nigerian constitution is very precise in its support for religion forming part of education. One way of trying to solve the problem is to allow the same conditions as operated with the take-over of primary schools to extend to post-primary institutions i.e. that the religion of the schools taken over should continue to be encouraged through co-operation between the former proprietors and the government. Alternatively, the government should prepare itself to provide teachers for the two major religions, i.e. Islam and Christianity, and post such teachers according to the needs of the children in different schools.

The effective implementation of the education ordinances in the past has been inhibited by finance and other such non-educational factors. The effect of these factors could be eliminated in future by educational legislation. For example, it is important to determine to what extent local customs inhibit the education of women in the Northern States. According to Mallama Hassu Iro Kaita, in the paper she submitted to the National Curriculum Conference, the problem of early child marriage is a serious impediment to the education of women in the far Northern States. She said:

> A girl may sit for the common entrance examination and get admitted to a secondary school after doing very well in examinations. Her parents may decide to withdraw her from going for further study; in this case, she is forced by local customs to get married at the age of twelve to thirteen sometimes to an old man. Of course at this stage the girl has not yet developed or even matured enough to shoulder her home responsibilities nor is she ready to bring up her own children. She is after all, a child herself, requiring parental care and guidance.[1]

The federal government should play a more co-ordinating role in matters of education. Curriculum workshops and reforms, research into educational problems and training and retraining of teachers are now going on in the different states to the extent that the 'left hand does not know what the right hand is doing'. This situation leaves much to be desired. There should be a clear demarcation of functions between the

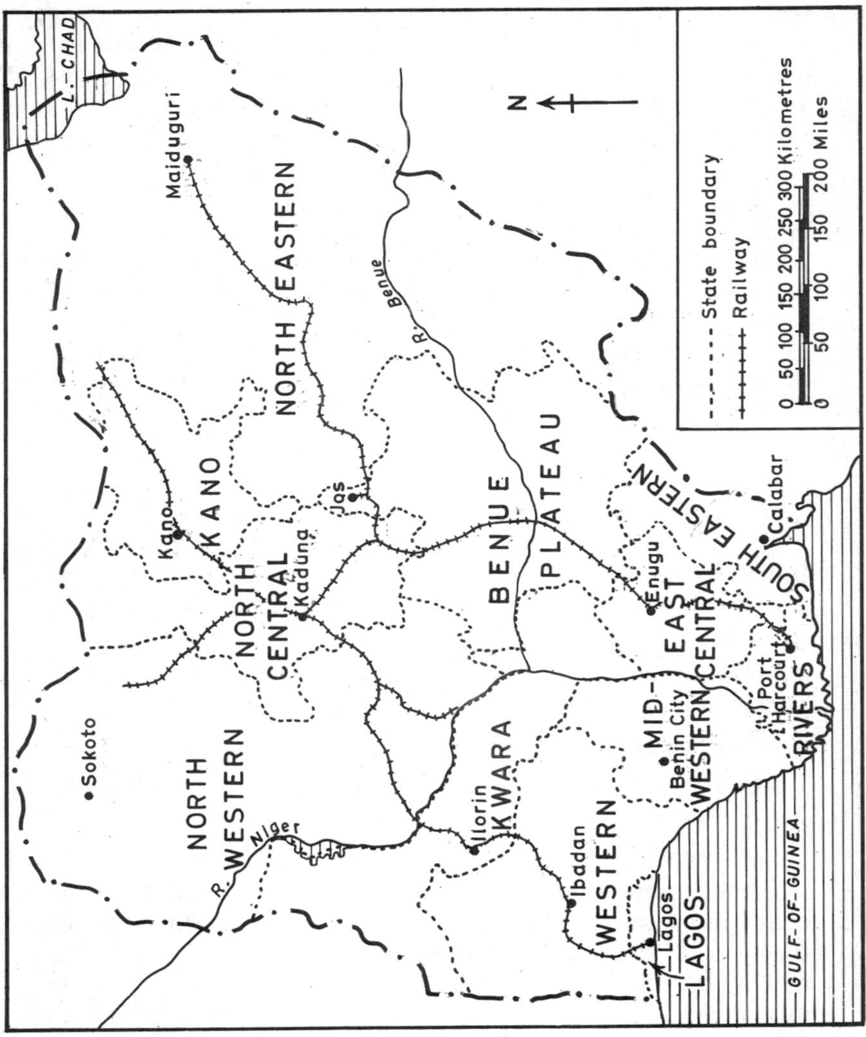
L.-CHAD
Maiduguri
NORTH EASTERN
KANO
Kano
Jos
NORTH CENTRAL
Kaduna
BENUE
PLATEAU
R. Benue
SOUTH EASTERN
Calabar
Enugu
EAST CENTRAL
Port Harcourt
RIVERS
MID-WESTERN
Benin City
NORTH WESTERN
Sokoto
R. Niger
KWARA
Ilorin
WESTERN
Ibadan
LAGOS
Lagos
GULF-OF-GUINEA
N
State boundary
Railway
0 50 100 150 200 250 300 Kilometres
0 50 100 150 200 Miles

federal and state ministries of education. A good question to ask to illustrate the point is whether it is necessary for both the federal and state governments to operate secondary schools (as at present) in each state. The contention at the moment is that the federal institutions are centres for promoting national unity. By deduction, the state institutions are therefore not such centres and could not be. Could the states not be encouraged to assume the role of promoting national unity in their schools as well?

At present some state governments have taken over the management of private schools, others have set up school boards to take over the managements of such schools, while yet other states are still operating the dual system of control by government and voluntary agencies. There should be a national policy in so important a matter as the education of the future citizens of Nigeria.

SECOND NATIONAL DEVELOPMENT PLAN

In 1970 the Federal Military Government promulgated the Second National Development Plan 1970-1974 in which five main national objectives were stated:[2]

(a) a united, strong and self-reliant nation;
(b) a great and dynamic economy;
(c) a just and egalitarian society;
(d) a land of bright and full opportunities for all citizens; and
(e) a free and democratic society.

In the same Development Plan, the performance of the education sector was limited to that of taking 'full account of the needs of the country in terms of developmental manpower and skills'. The major aim of educational policy was to be the ultimate provision of formal education to every child of school going age, at least up to the end of the primary school level. The objective was the creation of an adequate stock of the skills needed in the process of social and economic development.

If one bears in mind the wealth of information collected during the Curriculum Conference of 1969, the educational policies proposed in the Second National Development Plan cannot be regarded as full and adequate. For the immediate purpose of formulating measures to restore and re-activate educational facilities and services, especially in the war-affected areas, the policy as a short-term plan was very realistic. But for an effective long-range policy it was necessary to define more clearly the responsibilities for educational development in Nigeria.

Accordingly, the Federal Commissioner of Education, on the advice of his colleagues the States' Commissioners of Education, arranged for a seminar on 'A National Policy on Education', in June 1973. Some of the reasons for holding the seminar were given by the Federal Commissioner in his opening address:

(a) That Nigeria required a departure from the existing practice regarding the ownership, control and administration of our educational institutions, if the national interest was to be well served.

(b) That the democratization of education did not exist in this country, hence the enrolment ratio in educational institutions varied widely from State to State. It also varied rather widely from one level of education to another, and even more so as between male and female enrolment.

(c) There was an urgent need for re-evaluating the contents of the curriculum in Nigeria in order to make it job-oriented, and for speeding up the training of the much needed manpower in certain fields of human endeavour, and for introducing modern concepts of human dignity and individual responsibility.

(d) There was a need for a revision of the existing division of administrative responsibilities and functions between the federal, state and local governments, and the agencies as well as for a redefinition of their financial powers.

(*e*) The proper roles in the educational process of teachers, parents and the community needed to be reviewed.

With these guidelines, the seminar was held from 4-8 June 1973 and it produced a comprehensive report on what should constitute the national policy for education. The Chairman, Chief S.O. Adebo, has submitted his report for the consideration of the governments of the federation.[3]

LEGISLATION AND EDUCATION

Another significant landmark in Nigerian educational development was the decision of the Supreme Military Council to amend the Republican Constitution of 1963[4] by transferring to the Concurrent Legislative List the subject of education, (with the exclusion of higher education). It also transferred higher education (as defined in Item 10 of the Concurrent Legislative List) to the Exclusive Legislative List. It was the belief of the Federal Military Government that by this transfer of education to the Concurrent List, the nation would be able to plan a national education policy, a common education law and system, uniform conditions of service for teachers, and uniform standards and a greater mobility of the teaching force.

By transferring higher education to the Exclusive Legislative List, it was hoped that the Federal Government would have greater control over the establishment of new universities and that it would also be able to influence the existing ones to reflect national aspirations and goals.

On the whole, the overall effect of these two amendments has been that instead of remaining a residual or exclusively state subject, education has now assumed an immense national importance. If the rapid expansion of education is to be well co-ordinated and not haphazard, more participation by the federal government at all levels should be welcomed.

These are all changes that will surely influence the form of the future of education ordinances. May what is best for the education of the Nigerian child develop.

NOTES

1 Federal Ministry of Education, *Report of National Curriculum Conference* Lagos, Nigeria: Nigeria Educational Research Council, 1970.

2 Federal Ministry of Information, *Second National Development Plan 1970-74,* (Federal Government Printer, Lagos, 1970).

3 *Report of the Seminar on A National Policy on Education* (Academy Press Ltd. Lagos, 1973).

4 Federal Republic of Nigeria, *The Constitution of the Federal Republic of Nigeria* (Federal Ministry of Information, Lagos, 1963) p. 77.

F. Lugard

14th December, 1916.

No. L. **1916.**

Colony and Protectorate of Nigeria.

IN THE SEVENTH YEAR OF THE REIGN OF

HIS MAJESTY KING GEORGE V.

SIR FREDERICK JOHN DEALTRY LUGARD,

G.C.M.G., C.B., D.S.O.,

Governor-General and Commander-in-Chief.

An Ordinance relating to Education. Title.

[21st DECEMBER, 1916.] Date of commencement.

BE IT ENACTED by the Governor of the Colony and Protectorate of Nigeria, with the advice and consent of the Legislative Council so far as the provisions hereof relate to the Colony, as follows :— Enactment.

1. This Ordinance may be cited as the Education Ordinance, 1916. Short Title.

Definitions. **2.** Definitions :—

"The Board" means a Board of Education constituted under this Ordinance.

"School" means an institution in which more than ten pupils are systematically taught, and in which any person is engaged to impart education.

"Government School" means a school established by the Governor and maintained wholly or in part by the Public Revenue.

"Assisted School" means a school other than a government school to which, under the provisions of this Ordinance, a grant is made from Public Revenue.

"Manager" in the case of a school which is conducted by the proprietor in person means the proprietor, and in the case of every other school means the person for the time being appointed by the proprietor to be the responsible local representative of the proprietor.

"Proprietor" in relation to a school means any person, society or corporation by whom or which a non-government school is established or conducted.

"Staff" in relation to a school means all persons engaged in teaching in the school.

"Training Institution" means an institution for the training of teachers.

"Inspector" means an Inspector of schools appointed by the Governor.

Establishment of Government Schools. **3.** The Governor may from time to time establish Government Schools in Nigeria.

Any school established by the Government prior to the commencement of this Ordinance shall be deemed to be a Government School established under this Ordinance.

Constitution of Board of Education. **4.** (1) There shall be a Board of Education for the Colony and the Southern Provinces of the Protectorate, and also a Board of Education for the Northern Provinces of the Protectorate.

Such Boards shall be constituted as follows:—

Colony and Southern Provinces.	Northern Provinces.
The Lieutenant Governor. The Administrator. The Director of Education. The Principal Medical Officer and 4 other persons to be appointed by the Governor.	The Lieutenant Governor. A Resident to be nominated by the Governor. The Director of Education and 2 other persons to be appointed by the Governor.

The persons to be appointed by the Governor shall, so far as is possible, be selected from persons who are connected with Assisted Schools in the area for which the Board is constituted.

(2) Members appointed by the Governor may be appointed for any period not exceeding three years, and shall be eligible for re-appointment thereafter.

(3) The Lieutenant Governor or in his absence the next senior official member shall be President of the Board.

(4) The President and three other members shall form a quorum.

(5) In case of equality of votes the President shall have a casting vote in addition to his vote as a member.

5. A Board shall perform such duties as may be prescribed or as may be directed by the Governor and shall meet at the times and places appointed by the President who shall forward a report of the proceedings of each meeting to the Governor. Functions and meeting of the Board.

6. (1) The Governor may establish School Committees in the Colony and in any province of the Protectorate. School Committees.

(2) The Administrator shall be Chairman of the School Committees appointed for the Colony, and the Resident or Commissioner in charge of the Province shall be Chairman of the Committees appointed

for the Province, and the Committee shall consist of the Chairman and such persons as may be appointed by the Governor.

(3) When the Chairman is unable to attend a meeting of the Committee he may appoint some other member of the Committee to act as Chairman at such meeting.

(4) Three members of a Committee shall form a quorum.

(5) In case of equality of votes the Chairman shall have a casting vote in addition to his vote as a member.

Functions and meeting of Committee.

7. A School Committee shall perform such duties in relation to Government Schools and Assisted Schools in the area for which the Committee is appointed as may be prescribed or as may be directed by the Governor, and shall meet at such times and places as may be appointed by the Chairman, who shall forward a report of the proceedings of each meeting to the Director of Education.

The appointment of Manager of non-Government School.

8. The proprietor of every school (other than a Government school) which is not conducted by the proprietor in person, shall, in the case of a school established before the commencement of this Ordinance, immediately after the commencement of this Ordinance, and in the case of a school established after the commencement of this Ordinance, before the school is opened for the reception of pupils, appoint, and notify the Governor of the appointment of, some person connected with the school and resident in Nigeria to be the responsible local representative of the proprietor to whom any communication from the Government relating to the school may be addressed, and shall at all times thereafter have a representative and notify the Governor of any change either in the person or the address of his representative.

For a failure to comply with any of the requirements of this section the proprietor shall be liable to a fine of ten pounds.

9. (1) The Manager of every school shall send to the Governor in the month of January in every year a return showing the following particulars— Returns to be furnished to the Governor by the Manager.

(a) The name and address of the proprietor of the school.

(b) The name and address of the Manager.

(c) The situation of the school.

(d) Subjects taught or proposed to be taught in the school.

(e) Creed of the proprietor of the school and whether taught to the pupils.

(f) Number of pupils on the roll and average annual attendance of pupils.

(g) Number, qualifications and nationality of the staff.

(2) The Manager of a school shall be liable to a fine of ten pounds if he shall neglect to furnish a return required under subsection (1), and to a fine of one hundred pounds if he shall furnish a return in which any of the particulars are false to his knowledge.

10. (1) The Manager and the person for the time being in charge of every Assisted School shall permit the Director of Education or any Inspector to enter and inspect the school at any time, and shall furnish any information which the Director or Inspector may demand with regard to the care and tuition of the pupils, the names and qualifications of the staff and generally with regard to the management of the school. Inspection of Schools.

(2) The Manager or person in charge of an assisted school who shall refuse to permit the Director of Education or any Inspector of Schools appointed by the Governor to enter and inspect the school, or who refuses or neglects to give any information demanded as aforesaid, or who shall give any information which he knows to be false, shall be liable to a fine of ten pounds.

Grants from Public Revenue.

11. Subject to the provisions of this Ordinance and to the regulations any non-Government School or Training Institution shall, on application being made Government grant to school.

by the Manager thereof, be entitled to a grant from the Public Revenues of such amount and subject to such conditions as are prescribed by the regulations.

Grants how made.

12. No grant shall be made except on the recommendation of the Director of Education and with the consent of the Governor who may in any case alter any grant recommended by the Director of Education.

When grant is not to be made

13. No grant shall be made to any school or training institution—

(*a*) Which is self supporting or yields a profit to its proprietor;

(*b*) Which the Governor has reason to believe has reduced its school fees in consequence of the prospect of a grant;

(*c*) Which may be found to have presented a falsified register or return affecting the amount of the grant; or

(*d*) Which the Governor considers superfluous by reason of the proximity of a pre-existing school.

(*e*) Which is a Mission or other Christian school or training institution situate in a District of the Northern Provinces in which no Mission or other Christian school or training institution is established at the commencement of the Ordinance.

Refund of grant in certain cases.

14. The proprietor and manager of a school or training institution shall be jointly and severally liable to refund the whole grant made to a school or training institution if it should be found that the grant made was greater in amount than it should have been owing to any misrepresentation or false return wilfully and knowingly made by the proprietor or manager, and to refund any portion of a grant which was made in error and which should not have been made.

Miscellaneous.

15. The Governor in Council may make regulations for the purpose of giving effect to this Ordinance and in particular with regard to— Regulations.

(*a*) The functions and duties of the Board and of School Committee;

(*b*) The application for and the allowance of grants to Assisted Schools;

(*c*) The instruction to be given at Government and Assisted Schools;

(*d*) The examination of Government and Assisted Schools;

(*e*) The examination of persons to be employed as teachers at Government and Assisted Schools; the granting of certificates of competency to such persons; the classification of such certificates and the suspension or cancellation of certificates;

(*f*) The records, including account books, to be kept at Government and Assisted Schools, and the returns to be furnished by the managers of Assisted Schools;

(*g*) The religious or moral instruction to be given at Government and Assisted Schools;

(*h*) Prescribing rates of grants to Assisted Schools and Training Institutions;

(*i*) The relations between Schools and Government Departments in regard to apprentices;

(*j*) Generally for giving effect to the purposes of this Ordinance.

16. Nothing in this Ordinance shall be construed to prevent the Governor from making a direct grant from Public Revenue to any school. Governor may make special grant to schools and institutions.

17. The Education Ordinance (Chapter LXXV of the laws of Southern Nigeria) as amended by the Statute Laws Revision Ordinance No. 2 of 1908, is hereby repealed. Repeal.

This printed impression has been carefully compared by me with the Bill which has passed the Legislative Council, and, in so far as the provisions thereof relate to the Colony, is found by me to be a true and correctly printed copy of the said Bill.

Clerk of the Legislative Council.

Assented to in His Majesty's name in so far as the provisions hereof relate to the Colony, and enacted by me in so far as the provisions hereof relate to the Protectorate, this 14th day of December, 1916.

F. Lugard

Governor-General.

Printed by the Government Printer, Lagos. 14-12-16 6 [57]

BIBLIOGRAPHY

BOOKS

Ajayi, J. F. A., *Christian Missions in Nigeria 1841-1891,* London: Longman, 1965.

Akpofure, Rex, and Michael Crowder, *Nigeria—A Modern History for Schools,* London: Faber and Faber, 1966.

Armytage, W. H. G., *Four Hundred Years of English Education,* Cambridge University Press, 1964.

Ashby, Sir Eric, *Universities: British, Indian, African,* Cambridge, Massachusetts: Harvard University Press, 1966.

Awolowo, Obafemi, *The People's Republic,* Ibadan: Oxford University Press, 1968.

Bello, Alhaji Sir Ahmadu, *My Life,* Cambridge University Press, 1962.

Best, John W., *Research in Education,* 2nd ed. Englewood Cliffs, N. J.: Prentice-Hall, Inc., 1970.

Bittinger, Wright Desmond, *An Educational Experiment in Northern Nigeria in its Cultural Setting,* University of Pennsylvania, 1941.

Blitz, Franklin L., *The Politics and Administration of Nigerian Government,* London: The Eastern Press Ltd., 1965.

Bloch, Marc, *The Historian's Craft,* New York: Vintage Books, 1964.

Blum, Albert A., *Teacher Unions and Associations, A Comparative Study,* Urbana, Chicago: University of Illinois Press, 1970.

Burghardt du Bois, W. E., *The World and Africa,* New York: International Publishers. 1969.

Burns, A. C., *History of Nigeria,* London: George Allen and Unwin Ltd., 1963.

Burns, Donald G., *African Education,* London: Oxford University Press, 1965.

Butterfield, Herbert, *Man on His Past,* Boston: Beacon Press, 1966.

Canton, Norman F., and Richard I. Schneider, *How to Study History,* New York: Thomas Y. Crowell Company, 1967.

Coleman, James. S., *Education and Political Development,* Princeton, N. J.: Princeton University Press, 1968.

Collingwood, R. G., *The Idea of History,* London: Oxford University Press, 1969.

Cowan, Gray L., and others, *Education and Nation-Building in Africa,* New York: Frederick A. Praeger, 1965.

Dike, Onwuka, K., *100 Years of British Rule in Nigeria, 1851-1951,* Lagos, Nigeria: Federal Information Service, 1956.

________ *Trade and Politics in the Niger Delta, 1830-1885,* London: Oxford University Press, 1956.

Drury, Robert L., and Kenneth C. Ray, *Principles of School Law,* New York: Appleton-Century-Crofts, 1965.

Epelle, Sam, *Nigeria Speaks—Selected Speeches,* Nigeria: Longmans, 1964.

Elliot, William Y., *Education and Training in the Developing Countries,* New York: Frederick A. Praeger, 1966.

Ezera, Kalu, *Constitutional Development in Nigeria,* Cambridge University Press, 1960.

Frazer, Steward E., and William W. Brickman, *A History of International and Comparative Education,* Scott, Foresman and Co., 1968.

Garber, Lee O., *1962 Yearbook of School Law,* Danville, Illinois: The Interstate Printers and Publishers, Inc., 1962.

Geary, W. N. M., *Nigeria Under British Rule, New York:* Barnes and Noble, Inc., 1965.

Good, Carter, and others, *Methodology of Educational Research,* New York: Appleton-Century-Crofts, Inc., 1954.

Graham, Sonia F., *Government and Mission Education in Northern Nigeria, 1900-1919,* Ibadan University Press, 1962.

Hanson, John W., and Cole S. Brembeck, *Education and Development of Nations,* New York: Holt, Rinehart and Winston, 1966.

Hanson, John W., *Imagination and Hallucination in African Education,* Michigan: Michigan State University, Institute for International Studies, 1967.

Hazzledine, Douglas C., *The White Man in Nigeria,* New York: Negro University Press, 1969.

Herskovits, Melville J., *The Human Factor in Changing Africa,* New York: Random House, Inc., 1967.

Hilliard, F. H., *A Short History of Education in British West Africa,* London: Thomas Nelson and Sons Ltd., 1957.

Ikejiani, O., and others, *Education in Nigeria,* New York: Frederick A. Praeger, 1965.

Johnson, J. C. de Graft, *African Glory,* New York: Walker and Company, 1954.

Kent, Sherman, *Writing History,* 2nd ed. New York: Appleton-Century-Crofts, 1967.

Lewis, L. J., *Society, Schools and Progress in Nigeria,* Oxford: Pergamon Press, 1965.

——— *Educational Policy and Practice in British Tropical Areas,* London: Thomas Nelson and Sons Ltd., 1954.

——— *Phelps-Stokes Reports on Education in Africa,* London: Oxford University Press, 1962.

——— and A. J. Loveridge, *The Management of Education,* New York: Frederick A. Praeger, 1965.

Lugard, Sir F. D., *The Dual Mandate in British Tropical Africa,* Edinburgh: Blackwoods, 1923.

Mason, R. J., *British Education in Africa,* London: Oxford University Press, 1959.

Mellanby, Kenneth, *The Birth of Nigeria's University,* London: Methuen, 1958.

Miller, W. R. S., *Reflections of a Pioneer,* London: C.M.S., 1936.

——— *Have We Failed in Nigeria?,* London: Lutterworth Press, 1947.

Morphet, Edgar L., and Roe L. Johns, *Financing the Public Schools,* Englewood Cliffs, N. J.: Prentice-Hall, Inc., 1960.

Murray, A. Victor, *The School in the Bush,* London Longman's Green and Co., 1929.

Nduka, Otonti, *Western Education and the Nigerian Cultural Background,* Ibadan: Oxford University Press, 1964.

Nigerian Broadcasting Corporation, *Eminent Nigerians of the Nineteenth Century,* Cambridge University Press, 1960.

Niven, Sir Rex, *Nigerian,* New York: Frederick A. Praeger, 1967.

Nuffield Foundation and the Colonial Office, *African Education: A Study of Education Policy and Practice in British Tropical Africa,* Oxford University Press, 1953.

Orr, Sir Charles, *The Making of Northern Nigeria,* New York: Barnes and Noble, Inc., 1965.

Renier, G. J., *History, Its Purpose and Method,* New York: Harper Torchbooks, Harper and Row, 1965.

Reutter, Edmund E., and Robert E. Hamilton, *The Law of Public Education,* Mineola, New York: The Foundation Press, Inc., 1970.

Saunders, J. T., *University College, Ibadan,* Cambridge University Press, 1960.

Scalon, David G., *Church, State and Education in Africa,* Columbia University, New York: Teachers College Press, 1966.

——— *Traditions of African Education,* Columbia University, New York: Bureau of Publications, Teachers College, 1964.

Solaru, T. T., *Teacher Training in Nigeria,* Ibadan University Press, 1964.

Waugh, Auberon, and Suzanne Cronje, *Biafra: Britain's Shame,* London: Michael Joseph, 1969.

Williams, D. H., *A Short Survey of Education in Northern Nigeria,* Kaduna; Ministry of Education, Northern Region, 1960.

Wilson, John, *Education and Changing West African Culture,* London: Oxford University Press, 1966.

Wingfield, R. J., *The Saga of Lokoja's 100 Years: Features of the Northern Region of Nigeria,* Kaduna: Northern Nigeria Information of Service, 1960.

Wise, Colin G., *A History of Education in British West Africa,* London: Longman, Green and Co., 1956.

Zik, *A Selection from the Speeches of Nmandi Azikiwe,* Cambridge University Press, 1961.

PUBLICATIONS OF THE GOVERNMENT, LEARNED SOCIETIES AND OTHER ORGANIZATIONS

Ashby, Sir Eric, *Investment in Education–Report of the Commission on Post-School Certificate and Higher Education in Nigeria,* Lagos, Nigeria: Government Printer, 1960.

Colonial Office, *Colonial Annual Reports Nigeria 1947-1955,* London: H.M.S.O., 1956.

Central Office of Information, *Nigeria: The Making of a Nation,* London: Reference Division, Central Office of Information, 1960.

Colony and Protectorate of Nigeria, *An Ordinance to Consolidate and Amend the Law Relating to Education in Nigeria, 22nd May, 1952,* Lagos, Nigeria: Government Printer, 1952.

Colonial Office, *British Tropical Africa, The Place of the Vernacular in Native Education, Memorandum by the Advisory Committee on Native Education in Tropical Africa. African No. 1110,* London: Colonial Office, May, 1927.

——— *Advisory Committee on Education in the Colonies: A Preliminary Memorandum on the Aims and Methods of Language Teaching in the Colonies. Miscellaneous No. 411,* London: Colonial Office, 1930.

Director of Information Services, *Social and Economic Progress in the Northern Region of Nigeria,* Kaduna, Nigeria: Government Printer, 1955.

Education (Colony and Protectorate), *An Ordinance Relating to Education, 21st December, 1916,* Lagos, Nigeria: Government Printer, 1916.

Education (Northern Provinces), *No. 14 of 1926, An Ordinance Relating to Education in the Northern Provinces, 27th May, 1926,* Lagos, Nigeria: Government Printer, 1927.

Education, No. 39 of 1948. *An Ordinance to Make Better Provision in Regard to Education in Nigeria 1st January, 1949,* Lagos, Nigeria: Government Printer, 1949.

Federal Ministry of Education, *Statistics of Education in Nigeria 1965,* Lagos, Nigeria: The Federal Ministry of Information, Printing Division, 1965.

——— *Statistics of Education in Nigeria 1968.* Lagos, Nigeria, 1968.

——— *Educational Development 1961-70,* Lagos, Nigeria: Federal Government Printer, 1961.

——— *The Constitution of the Federal Republic of Nigeria,* Lagos, Nigeria: Federal Ministry of Information, Printing Division, 1963.

——— *Report of the Committee on the Grading of Duty Posts in Voluntary Agency Educational Institutions,* Lagos, Nigeria: Federal Ministry of Information, Printing Division, 1967.

——— *Grants in Aid of Education in Nigeria,* (Sir Sydney Phillipson), Lagos, Nigeria: Government Printer, 1949.

——— *Report of National Curriculum Conference 8th-12th September, 1969,* Lagos, Nigeria: Nigerian Educational Research Council, 1970.

Government Printer, *A ten-year Plan of Development and Welfare for Nigeria 1946,* Lagos, Nigeria: Government Printer, 1946.

——— *Memorandum on Educational Policy in Nigeria,* Lagos, Nigeria: Government Printer, 1947.

——— *Annual Report on the Education Department, 1935,* Lagos, Nigeria: Government Printer, 1936.

——— *Annual Report of the Education Department, 1st April, 1951 to 31st March, 1952,* Lagos, Nigeria: Government Printer, 1954.

———— *Annual Report of the Education Department, Northern Region, April, 1952 to March 1953,* Lagos, Nigeria: Government Printer, 1954.

———— *Annual Report of the Education Department, Northern Region, April 1953 to March 1954,* Lagos, Nigeria: Government Printer, 1954.

———— *Annual Report of the Education Department for the Year 1948,* Lagos, Nigeria: Government Printer, 1950.

———— *Annual Report on the Education Departments Northern and Southern Provinces for the Year 1929,* Lagos, Nigeria: Government Printer, 1930.

———— *Annual Report on the Education Department Northern Provinces for the Year 1928,* Lagos, Nigeria: Government Printer, 1929.

———— *Educational Problems and Progress in 1952. Northern Region of Nigeria,* Lagos, Nigeria: Government Printer, 1953.

———— *Speech and Address by His Excellency the Governor Sir Arthur Richards G.C.M.G., to the Legislative Council 18th March, 1946,* Lagos, Nigeria: Government Printer, 1946.

Government of Northern Nigeria, *A Special Speech by the Premier to All Institutions of Learning in Northern Nigeria,* Kaduna, Nigeria: Government Printer, 1963.

———— *White Paper on Education Development in Northern Nigeria,* Kaduna, Nigeria: Government Printer, 1961.

———— *Social and Economic Progress in the Northern Region of Nigeria,* Kaduna, Nigeria: Government Printer, 1955.

———— *Statement of Government Activities in the Northern Region,* Kaduna, Nigeria: Government Printer, 1959.

———— *Provincial Annual Reports 1963,* Kaduna, Nigeria: Government Printer, 1963.

———— *A Handbook for Inspectors,* Kaduna, Nigeria: Government Printer, Ministry of Education, Northern Nigeria, 1965.

———— *The Administration of Primary Education,* (H. Oldman), Kaduna, Nigeria: Government Printer, 1961.

———— *Annual Report of the Education Department of the Northern Region of Nigeria 1954-55,* Kaduna, Nigeria: Government Printer, 1956.

———— *Annual Summary of the Education Department of the Northern Region of Nigeria, 1955-56,* Kaduna, Nigeria: Government Printer, 1958.

———— *Annual Summary of the Education Department of the Northern Region of Nigeria 1956-57,* Kaduna, Nigeria: Government Printer, 1959.

———— *Development Plan 1962-68, Ministry of Economic Planning,* Kaduna, Nigeria: Government Printer, 1962.

———— *Development Plan 1962-68,* Kaduna, Nigeria: Government Printer, 1962.

———— *Steps on the Path of Progress—Ministry of Education,* Kaduna, Nigeria: Government Printer, 1965.

———— *Northern Regional Council House of Assembly Debates. Second Session, July 1948,* Kaduna, Nigeria: Government Printer, 1948.

———— *Northern Regional Council House of Assembly Debates. Second Session, February 1948,* Kaduna, Nigeria: Government Printer, 1948.

———— *Northern Regional Council House of Chiefs Debates, Second Session, February 1948,* Kaduna, Nigeria: Government Printer, 1948.

———— *The Education Law with Amendments up to 1st April, 1959,* Kaduna, Nigeria: Government Printer, 1959.

———— *The Education Law 1962 N. N. No. 43 of 1962,* Kaduna, Nigeria: Government Printer, 1962.

———— *Education Law of Northern Nigeria 1964,* Kaduna, Nigeria: Government Printer, 1964.

———— *Nigeria Gazettes, 1940-1968.*

Government of Western Nigeria, *Report of the Commission Appointed to Review the Educational System of Western Nigeria December 1960 to January 1961,* Ibadan, Nigeria: Government Printer, 1961.

Government of Eastern Region, *Annual Report of 1959,* Enugu, Nigeria: The Government Printer, 1961.

Hanson, John W., *Reports on the Supply of Secondary Level Teachers in English-Speaking Africa* (The Gambia, Swaziland, Botswana, Malawi, Lesotho, Tanzania), East Lansing, Michigan: Michigan State University, Institute for International Studies in Education and The African Studies Center, 1970.

Information Services, British, *Education in the United Kingdom Dependencies,* London: Reference Division 1.D.1193, September, 1954.

———— *Education in the United Kingdom Dependencies,* London: Cox and Sharland Ltd., 1959.

Masland, John W., *Educational Development in Africa: The Role of United States Assistance,* New York: Education and World Affairs, 1967.

Ministry of Economic Planning, *Statistical Yearbook 1966, Northern Region,* Kaduna, Nigeria: Baraka Press, 1966.

Ministry of Education, Planning and Development Division, Characteristics of Teachers in the Primary Schools of Northern Nigeria, 1963, Kaduna, Nigeria: Government Printer, 1964.

________ *Education in the Six Northern States of Nigeria 1962-72,* Kaduna, Nigeria: Baraka Press Ltd., 1967.

________ *School Directory for Northern States 1968,* Kaduna, Nigeria: Government Printer, 1968.

Phelps-Stokes, *Education in Africa. A Study of West, South and Equatorial Africa by the African Education Commission,* New York: Phelps-Stokes Fund, 1922.

Reports of the Third Commonwealth Education Conference 1964, Ottawa, Canada: Canadian Government Printing Bureau, 1964.

Report of the Fourth Commonwealth Education Conference 1968, Lagos, Nigeria: Commonwealth Secretariat, Parliament Building, 1968.

State of Ohio, *Laws and Regulations- Adopted by the State Board of Education December 11, 1961, Effective January 1, 1963,* Columbus: Department of Education.

UNESCO, *The Planning of Primary Education in Northern Nigeria,* J. F. Thornley, Paris 7e: International Institute for Educational Planning, Place de Fontenoy, 1966.

________ *The Integration of External Assistance with Educational Planning in Nigeria,* L. Cerych, 1966.

________ *The Organization of Educational Planning in Nigeria,* A. C. R. Wheeler, 1966.

________ *The Development of Higher Education in Africa,* 1963.

University of Wisconsin, *The Expansion of Teacher Education in Northern Nigeria 1961-1970,* University of Wisconsin, 1963.

United States National Commission for UNESCO, *A World to Gain: A Handbook for International Education Year, 1970,* Washington: National Education Association, 1969.

USAID, *Nigerian Human Resource Development and Utilization, Committee on Education and Human Resource Development, Nigeria Project Task Force,* New York: Education and World Affairs.

PERIODICALS

International, 'Nigeria: The Second Decade', *Newsweek* (October. 1970), pp. 44-46.

Nigeria Magazine, (1950-1960).

Reed, David, 'Nigeria—Black Africa's Brightest Hope', *The Reader's Digest* (March, 1963).

Rivlin, Alice M. 'Education, Politics and Federal Aid', *The Progressive* (October, 1970), pp. 31-36.

The Intercollegiate Review (Spring, 1970).

The Journal of Educational Thought, Vol. 3, No. 3 (December, 1969).

West African Journal of Education. (1968-1970).

NEWSPAPERS

Abubakar, Professor Iya, 'Role of Science and Technology in our National Development', *New Nigerian* 27 October 1969, p. 5.

Audu, Dr. Ishaya, 'Changes in the Curriculum', *New Nigerian,* October 28, 1969, p. 1.

Ogunsakin, Patrick, 'Focus on Education', *Morning Post,* 16 January 1970, p. 8.

Ogunsola, Albert F., 'Free Primary Education for Nigerian Children', *New Nigerian,* 18 September 1969, p. 5.

ESSAYS AND ARTICLES IN COLLECTIONS

Crowder, Michael, 'Nigeria—1960' *Nigeria Magazine, A Special Independence Issue,* pp. 5-13.

Galloway, A. D., 'Missionary Impact on Nigeria', *Nigeria Magazine, A Special Independence Issue,* pp. 59-60.

Kirk-Greene, A. H. M., 'Nigerian Explorers', *Nigeria Magazine, A Special Independence Issue,* pp. 66-73.

UNPUBLISHED MATERIALS

Ademuwagun, Zacchaeus Akingbade, 'An Investigation of the Relationship between Yoruba Culture and Formal Education in Nigeria', Unpublished Ed.D. Thesis, Boston University, 1965.

Essien, David Sam, 'A Resume of Financial Support of American Public Education and Its Implications for Education in Nigeria'. Unpublished Ph.D. Dissertation, University of Colorado, 1965.

Florin, Hans Wilhelm, 'The Southern Baptist Foreign Mission Enterprise in Western Nigeria, An Analysis', Unpublished Ph.D. Thesis, Boston University, 1960.

Ibok-Ete, Isong Uyo Nnanna, 'Education and Politics in Nigeria 1945-1960: A Comparative Study of the Educational Concepts of Selected Nigerian Political Leaders and Their Impact on Education'. Unpublished Ed.D. Thesis, University of California, Los Angeles, 1964.

Means, John E., 'A Study of the Influence of Islam in Northern Nigeria'. Unpublished Ph.D. Thesis, Georgetown University, 1965.

National Archives, Kaduna, 'Confidential No. 1279/1915'.

National Archives, Kaduna, 'Director of Education N.P., SNP. 9C. 119/1915, War Office, Whitehall, December 11, 1915'.

National Archives, Kaduna, 'Bonar, A. Law—A reply to Lord Lugard's extracts'.

National Archives, Kaduna, 'Lord Lugard—SNP8 File No. 87/1917, Extracts from F. D. Lugard, Governor-General's letter to the Right Honourable A. Bonar Law, P.C., M.P. Secretary of State for the Colonies, written in London dated 14th August, 1915'.

National Archives, Kaduna, 'H. Tugwell, Letter from Bishop Tugwell, Lokoja, Nigeria, October, 30, 1916'.

National Archives, Kaduna, 'Secretary, Northern Provinces, Reply to Bishop Tugwell, File No. SNP 8/4, 46/7, SM 1002/1916, Lokoja'.

Okeke, U., 'Educational Reconstruction in an Independent Nigeria', Unpublished Ph.D. Thesis, New York University, 1955.

Okongwu, N. J., 'History of Education in Nigeria, 1842-1942'. Unpublished Ph.D. Thesis, New York University, 1964.

Whitaker, Cleophaus Sylvester, Jr., 'The Politics of Tradition, A Study of Continuity and Change in Northern Nigeria 1946-60', Unpublished Ph.D. Thesis, Princeton University, 1964.

INDEX